Contents

Life-changing journeys

The journeys we embark on may change our lives, as we see in this quarter's readings. My life journey changed significantly when I responded to God's call to do an evangelistic gap year with Youth for Christ when I thought I was going to continue in teaching until retirement! We never know when God may intervene in our plans and take our journey in a direction we were not expecting. But we may also want to think about how our interactions with others have affected our journey, as well as remember those who have been companions on our journey and made a difference in our lives. We always need to remember, too, that in all of these journeys we are never alone. God is with us, as he was with those whose stories we will read about this quarter.

We continue our journey through Mark's Gospel with two sets of readings. The first mainly focuses on some of the different characters we meet along the way; the second more on what we can expect in life as disciples of Jesus. The readings from Isaiah encourage us to go on a journey of expanding our vision, trusting in God's faithfulness. As we grapple with the chapters in Romans, we find insights which inform our journey of discipleship and help us to know what is good to do and, conversely, what to avoid. We explore more of the story of Jacob in Genesis and read of his life-changing journey with God, including wrestling with an angel and getting a new name, Israel. It is encouraging to read that there are still glimpses of the impact of Paul's journeys in Acts to be seen today and it is exciting to see how the Holy Spirit led him. In reading Hosea, we will see the radical nature of God's love unfold as we follow his life-changing journey. The story of David continues in 2 Samuel and we encounter both one who is after God's own heart (1 Samuel 13:14) and a flawed hero who makes mistakes.

As you read this quarter's notes, think about what you can learn for your own life-changing journey from those encountered. Who do you most identify with? What stories might you be able to share with others to encourage or inspire them on their own journeys?

Sally Nash
Editor

Daily Bread toolbox

Sally Nash was originally a secondary school teacher. She has worked in ministry and theological education for many years, including with British Youth for Christ, St John's College Nottingham and St Padarn's Institute in Cardiff. Sally enjoys writing and has published a range of books and articles on different aspects of ministry, including work with children and young people. She is a practical theologian with research interests in shame, longevity in ministry and paediatric spiritual care. Sally is a self-supporting associate minister in an outer estate church.

WAY IN

This page introduces both the notes and the writer. It sets the scene and tells you what you need to know to get into each series.

A DAY'S NOTE

The notes for each day include five key elements: *Prepare, Read* (the Bible passage for the day), *Explore, Respond* and *Bible in a year.* These are intended to provide a helpful way of meeting God in his Word.

PREPARE

Prepare yourself to meet with God and pray that the Holy Spirit will help you to understand and respond to what you read.

READ

Read the Bible passage, taking time to absorb and simply enjoy it. A verse or two from the Bible text is usually included on each page, but it's important to read the whole passage.

EXPLORE

Explore the meaning of the passage, listening for what God may be saying to you. Before you read the comment, ask yourself: what is the main point of this passage? What is God showing me about himself or about my life? Is there a promise or a command, a warning or example to take special notice of?

RESPOND

Respond to what God has shown you in the passage in worship and pray for yourself and others. Decide how to share your discoveries with others.

BIBLE IN A YEAR

If your aim is to know God and his Word more deeply, why not follow this plan and read the whole Bible in one year?

Cascading faith

When a Samaritan woman met Jesus, it changed not just her life but the lives of all in her community too. SU's National Director Dave Newton explores what her story teaches us in revealing Jesus to children and young people today.

'... but whoever drinks the water I give them will never thirst. Indeed, the water I give them will become in them a spring of water welling up to eternal life' (John 4:14).

In the burning midday heat, a Samaritan woman heads to the well of Jacob to fill a jar with fresh water. As she approaches, she is surprised to see Jesus (as there is longstanding animosity between Jews and Samaritans) – but she does not turn back.

As the story of the woman at the well in John 4 unfolds, I think it highlights some important lessons for us as we seek to share Jesus with the next generation.

We need to go to where young people are

Most Jews going to Galilee would have gone round and not through Samaria. But Jesus chose to venture into this unfamiliar and perhaps uncomfortable territory so that the woman at the well could be the first non-Jew to hear that he was the long-foretold Messiah.

Some 95 per cent of children and young people today do not go to church, so we need to follow Jesus' example and go to them instead – even if sometimes that means going beyond our own comfort zone. We also need to know what to do once we get there!

So, Scripture Union offers resources and support to churches, helping them to reach and share the good news with young people in language they will understand.

Young people are thirsting for purpose

Jesus knows that the Samaritan woman is spiritually thirsty, that her life is unsatisfying. By asking her for water he makes that vital first connection and, given that he is a Jew, this intrigues her. She starts asking questions, and gradually Jesus reveals that he is the Messiah.

Children and young people have access to endless entertainment – online gaming, music, video streaming – but the gratification is fleeting. As our Faith Guides have witnessed, many are thirsting for a sense of purpose and identity that can only be found in God and are really open to exploring faith and responding to Jesus.

'It's like we're living in a revival!' says Southampton-based Faith Guide Carolyn, who has seen the two after-school clubs she set up in 2021 grow to 45 children and young people. 'The children begged us for Bibles, so the church donated some. Now they are reading them at home between sessions and asking lots of questions. They talk to their families about faith too – one mum told me, "We're not church people but my daughter keeps on about this Jesus!"'

In Newcastle, Faith Guide Joel Barwick reports that one lad on a residential had a vision of a glowing cross with angel wings, and heard a voice say, 'Jesus is here with you always; never forget he is coming – be prepared.' The boy later said, 'I wasn't really the believing type.

But now I know that God's real. And I feel like before the residential my brain was backwards, but now it's the right way round.' What a great description of how God transforms us!

Faith Guides Tabz and Hettie say children in Southport have prayed for healing and been healed. In Wales, Faith Guides Ruth and Lox say of their youth group, 'We have worship, Bible study and prayer, which our young people love – they are amazed they can speak to God and he hears!'

God is powerfully at work in the lives of children and young people.

Young people know Jesus is too good not to share!

When Jesus tells the Samaritan woman he is the Messiah, it immediately changes her priorities. She leaves her water jar at the well as she hurries back to her community to tell them to 'Come and see!' They follow her to Jesus and they too hear and accept his message.

Frequently, we find that young people who respond to Jesus don't just seek to quench their own spiritual thirst. They're eager to share his message of hope with others too. Scripture Union supports and trains them to do this confidently.

Some young Christians learn by volunteering on SU holidays and events. Lottie had no church background, but her mum took her to the local SU beach mission (Sutton-on-Sea) from a young age. Through that community, she found faith and later became a young leader. Lottie loves helping those children without church backgrounds to explore faith. 'I know that they can feel they are "different" from the other children. It's so rewarding when they ask questions and genuinely want to know more. And it's so gratifying to know that I'm the one they trust to tell them about Jesus.'

It was through Amplify Young Evangelists Academy, set up by Scripture Union and Christian youth partner organisations, that Lydia learned how to share her faith. Now she is a young leader on Amplify, supporting more recent intakes of students. At her university in York, she also regularly goes out with her church to share Jesus on campus.

She says, 'I realised our purpose is not just to be in a relationship with God but to tell others they can be too. The good news is too good to keep to ourselves!'

Young people are open to faith

Eleanor is a young leader on SU's Escape Holiday, having come to faith there a few years ago. She has also helped to shape our Young Leaders Development Programme, which gives young Christians the confidence to reveal Jesus to those around them. At university, Eleanor joins others from the Christian Union to share tea, biscuits and Jesus outside nightclubs on a Friday evening.

She says, 'People are so much more open to faith than I ever expected. They're missing out on that hope of Jesus. They're seeing all the brokenness of the world but they're not seeing how it's all going to be restored.

'If every single Christian stepped out and shared their faith, we could make a massive impact on those 12 million young people who don't know the gospel.'

Please pray with us

Praise God for all the children and young people he is drawing to himself from beyond the church walls, and for the churches and Faith Guides that are revealing Jesus to them.

Dave Newton

Give thanks for the vision and enthusiasm that God has given to all our young leaders. Pray that they will continue to grow in faith and confidence as they reveal Jesus to those around them, and for that to have a positive impact on the wider society.

Pray for God to continue to raise up many more young leaders and consider if you can give and support this vital work.

And finally, let's pray for our nation – may it once again turn to God and its people find their true purpose.

Play your part

Discover more about Scripture Union's mission to Reveal Jesus to children and young people, and see how you can get involved – practically or through your gifts and prayers – at su.org.uk/beyondbibleguides

Mark 6–8

Who does he think he is?

About the writer
Ro Willoughby

For many years Ro was a commissioning editor with Scripture Union. Now a lay minister in St Chad's Woodseats, Sheffield, she enjoys the many benefits of life in Sheffield, which include the company of family, friends, neighbours and fellow pilgrims.

The popular TV series *Who Do You Think You Are?* throws up many surprises for celebrities researching their family tree. The broadcaster Jeremy Paxman was deeply moved to hear that his indomitable great-great-grandmother raised her many children in abject poverty. Composer Andrew Lloyd Webber was delighted to unearth musical talent in his ancestry.

By the age of 12, Jesus had clearly realised his divine origins. He must have gradually grown aware of his identity and where his destiny lay. Some people who encountered him mockingly said, 'Who on earth does he think he is?' Others recognised something in Jesus they found attractive. Many chose to follow him.

These chapters in Mark's Gospel make us pause to wonder at how extraordinary it is for the God of this world to make 'himself nothing by taking the very nature of a servant, being made in human likeness' (Philippians 2:7). In writing this series I've reflected on how fascinating Jesus is in his deity and humanity. Some titles I've given him may seem disrespectful. This is not my intention, but simply to reflect on God as a fully rounded human being, a first-century Jewish Palestinian who, as God, fully identifies with those of us who are twenty-first-century citizens of heaven.

May you 'see' Jesus in a fresh way through these chapters in Mark's Gospel.

'Our God, contracted to a span, incomprehensibly made man.'*

*'Let Earth and Heaven Combine', Charles Wesley, 1707-1778

Tuesday 1 July
Mark 6:1–13

The elder brother

PREPARE

Who do you think Jesus is? What three roles or titles would you attribute to him?

READ

Mark 6:1–13

EXPLORE

Years ago, I heard Brother Andrew speak about some Christians under persecution in Eastern Europe. When questioned about why they were meeting, they replied, 'We're meeting with our brothers and sisters to hear the last will and testament of our elder brother.' In one sense that is very true! According to the writer of Hebrews, Jesus identified himself as a brother to those who 'are made holy' by God.

The people in the synagogue in Jesus' home town may be amazed at Jesus' eloquence and miracles, but this does not compel them to respect or believe him. 'He's very ordinary! We know all about him.' Their statements underline the fact that Jesus had truly become 'one like us', a son, with a skilled trade and named brothers and sisters. What became of his sisters, I wonder?

The people's lack of faith takes Jesus by surprise. He'd laid aside all the glory of heaven resulting in restrictions upon his exercise of power, though he can still bestow power upon his disciples to heal and cast out demons (v 13). He prepares them to expect rejection, just like him.

... Jesus is not ashamed to call them brothers and sisters.

Hebrews 2:11

RESPOND

We share the same father and have brothers and sisters in common. What could it mean for us in the next 24 hours to have Jesus as an older brother, taking responsibility for us?

Bible in a year: 2 Chronicles 33,34; Psalms 75,76

Wednesday 2 July

Mark 6:14–29

John's cousin

PREPARE

As you read this unsavoury story, focus on just how decadently corrupt, abusive and godless Herod is. What can God say to you through this story?

READ

Mark 6:14–29

EXPLORE

John the Baptist and Jesus were related through their mothers. Both became well known. John was an Elijah-type figure, as some people labelled Jesus (v 15). He looked to the future, since someone more powerful would follow him (1:7), he launched Jesus' ministry through baptism (1:9) and aroused such intense opposition that ultimately it led to a gory death. Jesus was more powerful than John. His teaching also aroused violent opposition ending in a cruel death and faithful followers buried his body too. Unlike John, Jesus truly was raised from the dead.

Herod Antipas, who ruthlessly ruled in Galilee, was fascinated by Jesus. He associated the cousins with each other, believing Jesus was John the Baptist raised from the dead. Herod was still guiltily plagued over John's beheading. Luke writes that Herod's wish to meet Jesus was only satisfied at Jesus' trial (Luke 23:8,9). Neither John nor Jesus courted fame or power. They knew the message from God they had to announce, calling people to live holy lives, to enter the kingdom of God. Their 'celebrity' status was costly.

> ... Jesus' name had become well known ... Herod ... said ... 'John, whom I beheaded, has been raised from the dead!'
>
> **Mark 6:14,16**

RESPOND

We too are called to holy living in our unsavoury and broken world. It may be costly. Ask for an opportunity today to be faithful to your calling to follow in Christ's footsteps.

Bible in a year: 2 Chronicles 35,36; Luke 1:39–80

Thursday 3 July
Mark 6:30–44

Foodbank provider

PREPARE

Imagine yourself walking with family and friends some distance to see this miracle-worker. What role would each play as you listen all day and are then fed well?

READ

Mark 6:30–44

EXPLORE

If you'd been in the crowd, what one thing might you always remember? The chase, anticipating where Jesus' boat would land? Spending time with Jesus all day and listening to his teaching? Feeling hungry and anxiously wondering how you'd get home? Watching Jesus give thanks, break bread and then everyone has enough to eat? Amazement at how much was left?

Throughout this day, Jesus reveals so much of his character, far more than just feeding over 5,000 people. He's a leader who desires to spend quality time with his followers (vs 30,31); the most compelling human being anyone could ever meet (v 33); a riveting teacher who shares the mind of God with those who will listen (v 34); a pastor with the power and compassion to meet human need (v 37); a miracle-worker who makes sure everyone is satisfied (v 42) with more than enough to go round (v 43) because of his generous heart. What else could you add to the list? (You might add, as John does, a popular figure who refuses to lead a revolt against the Roman authorities.)

Looking up to heaven, he gave thanks and broke the loaves.

Mark 6:41

RESPOND

Who does Jesus think he is? Take one of his characteristics revealed in this story. What does this aspect of Jesus mean to you as you pray and meet with him?

Bible in a year: Ezra 1,2; Luke 2

Friday 4 July

Mark 6:45–56

Water strider

PREPARE

Pause to reflect. What troubles you most about our polluted, broken world?

READ

Mark 6:45–56

EXPLORE

Where air meets water, liquid water molecules are attracted to one another. This creates surface tension, like an elastic membrane. Long-legged insects like water striders, spreading their weight over a larger area, don't break the water's surface. They appear to glide. (It's a bit more complicated!) Ever wondered how Jesus could walk on top of water? Did he get wet feet?

He sends his disciples out on the lake where they end up in a tempestuous storm, without him. In due course he strides towards them. Immediately the wind dies down. How come? At the beginning of time Jesus was involved in creating the world. He knows how water, surface tension and storms work.

More obviously, as God he can do what no human being can. His statement to the disciples, 'It is I' (v 50), the Greek saying 'I am', resonates with God's self-disclosure to Moses from the burning bush – 'I AM WHO I AM' (Exodus 3:14). The disciples have an advantage over Moses because it is Jesus who makes the Creator God visible, stepping onto water to be seen by them in their distress.

> But when they saw him walking on the lake, they thought he was a ghost. They cried out.
>
> **Mark 6:49**

RESPOND

We live amid a climate crisis. All creatures living in or relying on rivers and seas (including water striders) are affected. Yet the Lord of creation is with us. Cry out to him to have mercy on this beautiful but polluted planet.

Bible in a year: Ezra 3,4; Luke 3

Saturday 5 July
Mark 7:1–8

Rule interpreter

PREPARE

Are you a natural rule-keeper or do you find rules irksome?

READ

Mark 7:1–8

EXPLORE

A recent podcast compared hand-washing dishes with using a dishwasher. Which is more environmentally friendly, more effective, more costly, more convenient? The dishwasher won on all counts, but with conditions. It depends on washing on a longer wash but lower temperature, rinsing dirty plates in water first and only running a programme when full. I wasn't convinced! Who knows best?

In general, according to the Old Testament, the only specific washing instructions were for priests in their priestly duties (Exodus 30:19–21). Everyone else only became understandably unclean if, for example, they touched some form of bodily fluids (Leviticus 15:11). However, in Jesus' time, many of the Jewish authorities are less concerned with matters of hygiene than they are about ritual purity to maintain a distinctiveness from Gentiles and certain Jewish sects.

The Pharisees live with complicated cleanliness rules, which Jesus often breaks, about mixing with tax collectors (2:14) and Gentiles (5:1) – even touching corpses (5:41). Don't you love how he defends his disciples? Being God, he isn't bound by 'the tradition of the elders' (v 3). He authoritatively interprets the prophet Isaiah's words, calling out empty worship. He invites people to abide by the rules of the kingdom of God.

'You have let go of the commands of God and are holding on to human traditions.'

Mark 7:8

RESPOND

What attitudes in society do you currently struggle to understand in the light of the rule of God? Pray about that now.

Bible in a year: Ezra 5,6; Psalm 77

Sunday 6 July

Psalm 45

For a royal wedding

PREPARE

The institution of marriage has changed over the centuries and is hotly debated. The importance of faith within a marriage attracts less interest. Ask God to help you reflect on this.

READ

Psalm 45

EXPLORE

Every message on a wedding card contains warm, appreciative comments. The bride and groom are the prince and princess on this one day. This song is no exception. Possibly it is composed for King Solomon marrying yet another foreign wife. As such it is culturally freighted.

More is made of his virtues than hers. As God's representative he's challenged to rule well, being faithful to God (v 4) for his throne is ultimately God's (v 6). Solomon's descendants did belong to an eternal line, which is why the writer of Hebrews, when referring to Christ, quotes verses 6 and 7 (Hebrews 1:8,9).

The royal bride is told to reject the gods of her own people (v 10). Jezebel, King Ahab's wife, is one example of failing to do so for she turned her husband's heart away from the Lord to serve her foreign gods (1 Kings 16:31–33; 21:25,26). In sharp contrast, Ruth, another foreign bride, rejected the gods of her dead first husband and eventually gave birth to the royal line of David (Ruth 1:16).

Marriage today is different from this writer's understanding. For a start, in most countries, polygamy is unlawful. In Christian marriage husband and wife are both accountable to God and both are called upon to enable the flourishing of faith and trust in him (Ephesians 5:21).

Led in with joy and gladness, they enter the palace of the king.

Psalm 45:15

RESPOND

Pray for those preparing for their marriage.

Bible in a year: Ezra 7,8; Luke 4

Monday 7 July
Mark 7:9–23

Perceptive teacher

PREPARE

Reflect on Psalm 51:10: 'Create in me a pure heart, O God, and renew a steadfast spirit within me.'

READ

Mark 7:9–23

EXPLORE

Jesus hasn't finished with cleanliness regulations. He addresses the Pharisees, the crowd and his disciples. Notice his different approaches. With the Pharisees he compares the words of Moses to their regulations. Read verses 10–13 out loud to capture Jesus' accusatory 'You'. Righteously forceful, he has swept away their traditions which have the opposite effect from their original intention. He is criticising the Pharisees for their focus on complying with the law in a way that negates the spirit of the law, through withholding support for parents. Thus, they dishonour their parents, breaking God's fifth commandment.

Jesus addresses the crowd, which may or may not have included his accusers. He wants everyone to understand something radically challenging. By eating with unclean hands (v 2) his disciples would never have made themselves unclean inside. Impurity is harboured in the inner being (v 15).

Finally, to explain how impure thoughts can lead to a long list of destructive behaviour, he takes his disciples aside. They are among those who are most receptive to his teaching. He knows what he needs to say. He doesn't shy away from speaking the hard truth.

Again Jesus called the crowd to him and said, 'Listen to me, everyone, and understand this.'
Mark 7:14

RESPOND

Pray for those who preach God's Word week by week. Following Jesus' example, they need God's wisdom not only to discern what comes from a pure heart in what they say, but also to assess the receptivity of their audience.

Bible in a year: Ezra 9,10; Luke 5

Tuesday 8 July

Mark 7:24–30

A friend of Gentiles

PREPARE

Remind yourself of how the Pharisees respond to Jesus in verses 1 to 23. Ask God to help you marvel at today's contrasting response to him.

READ

Mark 7:24–30

EXPLORE

Jesus has swept aside the regulations of the Pharisees. Now, probably wanting to escape their fierce opposition and maybe even Herod's sinister interest in him (6:14), he travels to the Gentile area around Tyre, on the coast of modern-day Lebanon. Mark even suggests Jesus wants to hide (v 24). In Jewish eyes, he is discovered by the most unacceptable person possible – an 'unclean' woman, a Greek Gentile, from the deeply pagan area of Syrian Phoenicia.

She hasn't come to criticise. All that comes out of her heart (v 21) is a desperate and bold request. Jesus tells her she is not a priority and even infers she's a dog. (The Greek word suggests a little dog, like a pet.) Astonishingly, she's not offended but accepts his primary Jewish calling, yet claims her own right to his attention. What a contrast to the hostility of the Jews!

Her daughter is restored to wholeness. Far more than that, Jesus has forever commended her with the words, 'Woman, you have great faith!' (Matthew 15:28). Martin Luther wrote, 'She took Christ at his own words. He then treated her not as a dog but as a child of Israel.'*

> Then he told her, 'For such a reply, you may go; the demon has left your daughter.'
>
> **Mark 7:29**

RESPOND

Jesus, knowing this woman's background, still accepts her and gives her far more than she expected. Pray for anyone you know who feels second-class in God's eyes, asking that they hear Jesus' words of acceptance and affirmation.

*R Bainton, *Here I Stand: A Life of Martin Luther*, Nashville: Abingdon, 1950, p362

Bible in a year: Nehemiah 1,2; Psalm 78:1–37

Wednesday 9 July
Mark 7:31–37

Hoped-for healer

PREPARE

Can you imagine the day when the glory of the Lord is finally fully revealed?

READ

Mark 7:31–37

EXPLORE

Jesus now travels 120 miles into Gentile territory, going up the Mediterranean coast to Sidon, then down to the ten Graeco-Roman cities, east of Lake Galilee. Maybe he wants a break from his Jewish critics.

His fame has gone ahead of him. People bring a deaf-mute man for Jesus to touch (v 32). In need of privacy, Jesus leads the man away from the crowd. Once more, Jesus becomes ritually 'unclean', engaging with and touching a Gentile man, then placing spit upon his tongue. The man must have seen Jesus looking to heaven, the source of his power to heal, but hears nothing until... he hears Jesus' voice and his own!

The Greek word for 'could hardly talk' (v 32) only appears once more in the Bible, in the Greek Septuagint (the Greek Old Testament), in Isaiah 35, a chapter that rejoices in the future day when the glory of the Lord will be revealed.

In earlier chapters, God's wrathful judgement upon Israel's neighbours has been foretold, nations that have defied God. Is Mark presenting Jesus, the restorer of speech and hearing, as the beginning of the fulfilment of that expected day of the Lord when Jews and Gentiles alike will see God's glory?

> ... they will see the glory of the LORD ... the ears of the deaf unstopped ... the mute tongue shout for joy.
>
> **Isaiah 35:2,5,6**

RESPOND

God still heals today. Occasionally someone's hearing is restored. For many deaf people, deafness is part of their identity. But on the day of the Lord nothing will hinder their hearing or speech. Pray for anyone you know who's deaf.

Bible in a year: Nehemiah 3,4; Luke 6

Thursday 10 July

Mark 8:1–13

Crowd controller

PREPARE

Why do you think the story of feeding the 5,000 is better known than the feeding of the 4,000? Ask God to speak to you today.

READ

Mark 8:1–13

EXPLORE

When attending a large sporting event or a festival, I'm aware of being organised. Officials speak into walkie-talkies; certain routes are closed off; notices dictate crowd behaviour; tickets are checked; bags are searched; cameras are everywhere!

Unlike in the feeding of the 5,000, Jesus makes the first move in taking charge of the crowd of 4,000. He notices they are hungry after having been with him three days – a devoted, long-suffering crowd in a remote spot, probably still in a Gentile region. He cares very deeply for them (vs 2,3). What do you notice about how Jesus relates to this crowd? Why hasn't he observed their hunger earlier? Did they not intend to stay so long?

He provides for their well-being. They are satisfied (v 8). We don't know what this crowd make of his teaching, unlike the crowd of 5,000 (John 6:15). But he doesn't dictate how they choose to respond. His return across the lake, to be confronted yet again by his Jewish critics, emphasises that Jesus does not control how people believe in him, whether Jew or Gentile. Note, he himself refuses to be controlled. He won't provide proof of his identity to order.

> The people ate and were satisfied. Afterwards the disciples picked up seven basketfuls of broken pieces that were left over.
>
> **Mark 8:8**

RESPOND

Pray for someone you know who is a Christian but finds it difficult to accept Jesus' compassion for them, or for someone who has not yet put their trust in him.

Bible in a year: Nehemiah 5,6; Luke 7

Friday 11 July
Mark 8:14–21

Disappointed mentor

PREPARE

Are you good at recognising where God's at work? Are you slow to connect the Word of God with your everyday life? Is anything obstructing your growth in faith?

READ

Mark 8:14–21

EXPLORE

Some people take to driving a car as the proverbial duck takes to water, others are almost paralysed by anxiety, others are just slow to learn and build up confidence, while some never learn.

Jesus is disturbed by the Pharisees' blank refusal to give him a fair hearing (v 12) and he's frustrated by the disciples' slowness to understand. Is there a difference between the two? On Tuesday we read how he probably travelled north to get away from the unbelief and rejection of the Pharisees and Herod. Here he's not deserting his disciples but longing for them to make progress in understanding.

Ironically this discussion begins because one loaf of bread is not enough to feed a boatful. Someone has forgotten to bring the lunch. They've all forgotten Jesus is in the boat. They've all forgotten how Jesus can provide enough bread for all. Would Jesus perform another miracle, or find another solution? We don't know. Like the Pharisees who are bound by material regulations, the disciples are bound by material things, not the spiritual bread of life. They are slow learners, spiritually short-sighted.

> ... Jesus asked them: 'Why are you talking about having no bread? Do you still not see or understand? Are your hearts hardened?'
>
> **Mark 8:17**

RESPOND

A few Pharisees put their faith in Christ. Filled with the Holy Spirit after Pentecost, Jesus' disciples were emboldened in faith. Pray for yourself and anyone you know who's a slow learner when it comes to trusting Jesus.

Bible in a year: Nehemiah 7,8; Luke 8

Saturday 12 July

Mark 8:22–26

Hands-on healer

PREPARE

Read Mark 6:1 to 8:21 again to remind yourself of your reflections in Mark.

READ

Mark 8:22–26

EXPLORE

As I've written these notes, I have noticed how the Gospel-writer finds links between incidents and the words of Jesus. For example, he traces the theme of rejection and unbelief with opportunities for Gentiles to hear Jesus' message and not just Jews. He includes two contrasting feeding miracles. This sight-restoring story relates to the blindness of faith in the previous discussion and also Wednesday's hearing restoration story (7:31–37). These two healing miracles are the only ones in Mark that don't also appear in Matthew and Luke. What similarities are there between the two?

In Mark's Gospel, Jesus lays his hands on or touches someone more than in any other Gospel. In all but one case it's in the context of healing. Here, rather beautifully, he privately takes the man by the hand. Then he touches his eyes in two stages, initially applying his spit. (Saliva was recognised as having healing properties.) Unlike in 7:34, he doesn't command the man to see. Unusually, he asks a question in the style of those in 8:17–21, as though probing the man's experience and understanding.

Is Mark presenting Jesus' question here (v 23) as one he might ask of anyone, Jew or Gentile? 'Do you see anything?' Partial vision can turn into faith-filled clarity.

> He took the blind man by the hand ... When he had spat on the man's eyes and put his hands on him, Jesus asked, 'Do you see anything?'
>
> **Mark 8:23**

RESPOND

This is the last reflection on these chapters of Mark's Gospel. If Jesus were to ask you, 'Have you seen anything?', what would you say?

Bible in a year: Nehemiah 9,10; Psalm 78:38–72

Sunday 13 July
Psalm 46

The eye of the storm

PREPARE

How troubled are you by current global challenges to life on earth? Are you tempted to wonder if God is powerless?

READ

Psalm 46

EXPLORE

Our ears and eyes are regularly assaulted by evidence of climate crisis: drought, floods, famine, mudslides, melting polar icecaps, rising sea levels, changing weather patterns. Recent wars have released global insecurity and cataclysmic devastation. We are faced with malign forces of nature and the brutal forces of war. Psalm 46 could well be describing our world (vs 1–3,6). The psalmist is not urging people to have faith in God but is raising the question whether the God they have put their faith in can be trusted. What evidence for confidence do you find here?

Interestingly, the Hebrew for 'break of day' (v 5) is the same phrase for the time Moses called the walls of the Red Sea to collapse (Exodus 14:27), evidence of God's power over both the natural world and the might of the enemy, in this case, the Egyptian army. Moses' and Miriam's subsequent songs graphically describe God's power (Exodus 15:7–11,21). This psalm has other resonances with that Red Sea escape.

God calls us to be still, to experience his presence in the eye of the storm, a refuge in the centre of a hurricane.

The LORD Almighty is with us.

Psalm 46:11

RESPOND

Hold out both hands. In your mind, place in one a war zone that troubles you, in the other a natural disaster that distresses you. Plead with God to intervene. Then hold out empty hands to receive God's powerful stillness.

Bible in a year: Nehemiah 11,12; Luke 9

REVEALING JESUS
95% of under-18s don't go to church.
So let's *Reveal Jesus* where they are!
PLAY YOUR PART:
su.org.uk/revealingjesus

Isaiah 46:1 – 51:16

Hold on tight!

Prophets announced their message publicly to whoever would listen. The book of the prophet Isaiah, commonly known as the 'fifth Gospel', can be divided into three sections, each with a particular theme or flavour and therefore with its own distinct tone. Although there are questions concerning the authorship of the book, a number of linguistic, structural and thematic features suggest its overall unity in the prophetic tradition. The book must be understood in the context of the exile – before, during and after. In this series, we will be delving deeper into 'Second Isaiah': the book of comfort.

Isaiah brings the message of the 'Holy One of Israel' to his people. The message is one of comfort and hope to a people who are beaten down, tempted and oppressed. Could it be true that rescue and release are at hand or even possible? Although Isaiah delivers a message of restoration, it is not without challenging words: an unfaithful, unbelieving nation that has lost sight of its role in the world, tensions between God and Israel have become apparent.

As you read Isaiah, sit with the prophet's words, no matter how sharp and prickly they might be, not forgetting the message that he wants to deliver: God's faithfulness and goodness have been tasted, which means that he can be trusted for the future. Be prepared to broaden your horizons and extend your vision!

About the writer
Nudrat Malik

A Pakistani Christian immigrant, Nudrat has only recently started describing herself as Asian British, despite having lived in England for most of her adult life. She lives with her family in Buckinghamshire, where she enjoys a recently discovered love of gardening.

Monday 14 July

Isaiah 46:1–13

Me, mine, myself

PREPARE

Listen to any contemplative or instrumental music of your choice.

READ

Isaiah 46:1–13

EXPLORE

The human condition is such that we have an overwhelming desire to control and order things our way. In a modern, busy and sometimes chaotic life, it is much easier to deal with the gods that we construct and control. The notion of a personal God who is relational brings with it demands and unpredictability, which may be too much to handle. The gods of our own making, depicted in our own way, using our own treasures – surely this is what we want: a situation in which we are at the centre. We become gods! These gods give us comfort because we can see them where we put them, we control them, we put them in a box: predictable and comfortable.

And that is exactly the opposite of what our Creator, Saviour God is! He is a personal God who responds to us, has a relationship with us (v 4). This passage is an invitation to identify those gods that we have chosen, shaped, decorated and then put in a spot of our choosing, going to any lengths to maintain our control. Isaiah wants us to acknowledge all those situations when we put ourselves in control, and to reflect on what it is that we fear facing.

> ... they set it up in its place, and there it stands. From that spot it cannot move. Even though someone cries out to it, it cannot answer; it cannot save them from their troubles.
>
> **Isaiah 46:7**

RESPOND

Make a list of things, situations or habits that put you in control. These may be leaving little room for a relational God in your everyday life. Say out loud: 'May your kingdom come in my life.'

Bible in a year: Nehemiah 13; Luke 10

Tuesday 15 July
Isaiah 48:1–11

Faithfulness to obedience

PREPARE

Recall some of the good things God has done in your life.

READ

Isaiah 48:1–11

EXPLORE

If the Scriptures tell us about God, they also tell us about ourselves and our humanity: broken, damaged, fickle and ungrateful. In Isaiah's words, the Holy One of Israel is trying to prove himself to the house of Jacob by telling the 'new' and 'unknown' things to come because they have failed to recognise who he is and what he has done. This zealous defence shows God to be one who tests, is patient, yet jealous. With its tendency to take control, Israel seems to have forgotten its relationship to the Lord Almighty. Are we any different?

Eugene Peterson in his introduction to the book of Isaiah in *The Message* writes, 'Isaiah involves taking the stuff of our ordinary and often disappointing human experience and showing us how it is the very stuff that God uses to create and save and give hope... nothing is unusable by God.' Could it be that we too have forgotten to recall the experiences of our lives which are an essential witness to God's faithfulness? May it be that reliving something jubilant or traumatic imprints the important message deep within: the Holy One is faithful and able to save!

For my own name's sake I delay my wrath; for the sake of my praise I hold it back from you, so as not to destroy you completely.

Isaiah 48:9

RESPOND

Look at a photo or postcard of an occasion – happy or sad – a trip, or a person. Is it possible to share this with your close family so that the blessing can be remembered or relived?

Bible in a year: Esther 1–3; Psalm 79

Wednesday 16 July

Isaiah 48:12–22

If only...

PREPARE

Use silence to still yourself: calm your breathing and wait for your heartbeat to find a comfortable rhythm.

READ

Isaiah 48:12–22

EXPLORE

It's clear that God lives with a huge 'if only' in his relationship with Israel. If only... if only Israel had listened and believed the one who 'laid the foundations of the earth' and told them 'these things' (vs 13,6). This refrain rings out clearly in this passage. The Holy One of Israel is trying to prove that he is God Almighty, one who should not be ignored. Yet, Israel continues to overlook her redeemer, the Lord.

Here, Isaiah brings his message to the people by explaining the loss they have had to experience; they have forfeited the blessings that would have been theirs. Isaiah is pointed but plain – Israel herself has become the biggest hindrance to experiencing continual and numberless blessings because she has failed to acknowledge God in relation to her very existence; yet he continues to appeal to them! In the words of Jo Bailey Wells, 'God neither insists on his way nor desists from loving them'.*

Now that this tug-of-war relationship is exposed, Isaiah makes it clear that one party is never going to give up in his faithfulness: the Holy One of Israel.

Listen to me, Jacob, Israel, whom I have called: I am he; I am the first and I am the last. My own hand laid the foundations of the earth, and my right hand spread out the heavens; when I summon them, they all stand up together.

Isaiah 48:12,13

RESPOND

Think about the image of a taut rope being pulled by God on one side and you on the other. Linger here for a while. What have you realised about yourself?

*J Bailey Wells, *Isaiah: The People's Bible Commentary*, Bible Reading Fellowship, 2006

Bible in a year: Esther 4,5; Luke 11

Thursday 17 July
Isaiah 49:1–13

God's justice on earth

PREPARE

Read Psalm 136 in two different translations.

READ

Isaiah 49:1–13

EXPLORE

This is a picture of redemption, of salvation; one that is extended to all and encompasses all, especially the beaten down, afflicted ones. It is a hope-filled passage for those who have faced challenging times. One cannot ignore the very physical nature of the afflictions: captives, those in darkness, hungry and thirsty (vs 9,10), all things that we still see. Food larders, pantries and food banks may be part of how redemption is announced to those who need it today and the reality of the world is that it is unjust for so many.

Many faith-based communities, for example churches, mosques and gurdwaras have become experts in attending to physical needs but sometimes have been hesitant to ask the more pertinent questions about the afflictions: captives of what? What is the nature of the darkness? Hungry and thirsty for what? It may be that redemption is on offer in the here and now only when systemic injustices are put right and through it the image of God is restored in each one of us.

Today's passage ends with a note of hope: God comforts his people and has compassion on those who suffer (v 13), he is a gracious God.

> ... the LORD comforts his people and will have compassion on his afflicted ones.
>
> **Isaiah 49:13**

RESPOND

Listen, really listen, to the captive who has just been freed, or that person who has stepped out of darkness, or someone who is hungry. Reflect on the image of God being restored in you both.

Bible in a year: Esther 6,7; Luke 12

Friday 18 July

Isaiah 49:14–26

Unbelievable!

PREPARE

Listen to one of the following pieces of music using an online search facility: 'The Lark Ascending' by Ralph Vaughan Williams; or 'A Change Is Gonna Come' by Sam Cooke.

READ

Isaiah 49:14–26

EXPLORE

Impossible things are done: exile to restoration. Unbelievable things happen because of the sovereign Lord. In this passage, Isaiah urges the reader to look beyond the current painful experience and keep an upward, hopeful perspective on things. The people felt that God had forgotten and forsaken them (v 14) but God never forgets us: as 2 Timothy 2:13 reminds us, God remains faithful even when we are faithless.

Living in the moment, being present with all our senses, is one way to manage and counter anxiety. But it could be argued, there are times when living in the moment, being present in the here-and-now, does no good. Think of someone who has had to live through traumatic times because of the actions of others.

I wonder if it would be beneficial or wholesome for them to linger in that present reality? We know that people need to move forward and look ahead. And yet, the trauma of a situation must have been an ever-present companion as it seemed to be with the children of Zion. In such circumstances we should hold fast to the hope that God, the Redeemer, will prevail (vs 25,26). Unbelievable things can happen, and will happen, because of the Sovereign Lord who is prepared to make them happen!

> ... captives will be taken from warriors, and plunder retrieved from the fierce; I will contend with those who contend with you, and your children I will save.
>
> **Isaiah 49:25**

RESPOND

Recall a time when something seemingly impossible or unbelievable happened, and thank God for what he did and who he is.

Bible in a year: Esther 8–10; Luke 13

Saturday 19 July
Isaiah 51:1–16

Awake, awake!

PREPARE

Read Psalm 139 in full.

READ

Isaiah 51:1–16

EXPLORE

I wonder if this passage brings any comfort to those who are living in constant fear, those who experience the wrath of the oppressor who is bent on destruction. If this text tells us anything, it is a description of the world as it is: where people experience the injustice of living in fear, where one human being will oppress another just because they are determined to do so, and where death is a reality that brings everything to an end.

As surely as this reality needs to be acknowledged, so does the salvation of the Lord who seems equally bent on working out his rescue plan, a way to rebuild that which is destroyed, restore that which is fruitless. In this, the physical earth is not forgotten: deserts are made into Eden, wastelands into gardens (v 3). If there ever was a call to keep perspective when things go wrong, this is it! These prophetic writings are here so that we can remember what the important things are. Isaiah, like the other prophets, brings a new awareness of the reality of God's involvement in everyday life – not bound by our definition of time and space. Justice, light, righteousness and hope are words used here to remind us of what salvation will look like.

> For the moth will eat them up like a garment; the worm will devour them like wool. But my righteousness will last for ever, my salvation through all generations.
>
> **Isaiah 51:8**

RESPOND

What role, if any, are you playing or are willing to play – in partnership with God – to bring about justice, light and comfort?

Bible in a year: Job 1,2; Psalm 80

Sunday 20 July
Psalm 47

Celebrate!

PREPARE

Read the Psalm using *The Message* translation; then read it again in a different translation.

READ

Psalm 47

EXPLORE

This psalm declares, in very definite human terms, that God is king. We are called to celebrate his kingship as we would any other victory: clap your hands, sound the trumpet, shout praise. Not only this, the victory is also portrayed in language that announces the complete and overpowering rule of the Lord Most High (v 2).

If the God of the Psalms – this very particular Jewish literary genre – is king, what does it mean for us in the here and now? Top of your list may be a cessation of wars around the world, as we are increasingly aware of the injustice of such all-encompassing conflict. Closer to home, you may be able to identify a neighbourhood dispute, the result of which is injustice faced by particular people and places. Advocating for those without a voice may be the start of God's rule.

The psalm declares God as 'king of all the earth'. What does this victory mean for the whole of creation? A stop to the destruction of nature – plants and habitats – may feature in your mind.

Let true victory be as the domino effect that brings about the righteous rule of God in the world: restoration for all of creation so that it can be declared 'good', as in the beginning of the world.

Clap your hands, all you nations; shout to God with cries of joy.

Psalm 47:1

RESPOND

'Sing your best song to God' (v 6, *The Message*). Which song would you sing, given the challenges of life for you at the moment? Use this suggested song* to celebrate with *all* of God's creation!

*The Lost Words – Spell Songs, https://www.youtube.com/watch?v=Hg1xFYpXuWA

Bible in a year: Job 3,4; Luke 14

WAY IN

Romans 12–16

Love practically

When the Christians at Rome first received Paul's letter to the Romans, I wonder if they settled down to listen to it in one session. It would have been quite a heavy session, requiring great powers of concentration! Or did they break it up into, say, three sessions? If so, the last third of the letter, which is the five chapters we are looking at, would have been the most practical and the easiest to follow.

About the writer
Roger Combes

Roger has ministered in parishes in London, Cambridge and Hastings, and as an archdeacon in West Sussex. Now retired, he and his wife Christine live in Crawley with good views of planes from London Gatwick. They have two daughters and two energetic grandchildren.

These chapters come after Paul has been explaining God's good news of Jesus Christ in some detail. Then Paul takes a big breath and says, 'Therefore...' (12:1). He spells out in straightforward language how he expects Christians to respond. He urges us all to live consistent lives of distinctive Christian character. In other words, the theme of our readings is, one way or another, 'love': loving behaviour towards our fellow believers, our neighbours and even our enemies.

This love that Paul speaks of is genuine and active. It includes being a team player in the church and a good citizen in the state. It is strong under pressure and gentle with the sensitive. It is discerning, principled and disciplined. It is warm-hearted and affectionate. And, as the letter comes to an end, the great apostle begins to step out of the pages and meet us as a sympathetic, caring and very human Christian leader.

Monday 21 July

Romans 12:1–8

Responding to God

PREPARE

'Come!' is the gentle but firm invitation from the Lord to us. As you come to the Bible today, also come to the Lord himself.

READ

Romans 12:1–8

EXPLORE

'I think what you need is Romans chapter 12 verse 1.' No one had ever spoken to me like that before. I was a typical 15-year-old with an uncomplicated trust in Christ. I was on a Christian skiing holiday, and the leader and I were having a chat. I was curious to discover what he meant, and we looked up Romans 12:1 together. I read that I needed to make a present of myself to God.

This is what the apostle Paul was looking for from the Christians in Rome in response to all God's mercies (v 1). The simple act and attitude of giving ourselves to God expresses the gratitude of our hearts and releases us to act on it in our lives. We shall find we can have a sturdy independence from the attitudes of the world around us (v 2), a more objective assessment of ourselves (v 3) and a much greater usefulness in the mission and ministry of Christ's church (vs 4–8).

When it comes to using our abilities and gifts in God's service, Paul urges that we play our part and do it with heart and soul. And that includes 'generously', 'diligently' and 'cheerfully' (v 8).

> Therefore, I urge you, brothers and sisters, in view of God's mercy, to offer your bodies as a living sacrifice, holy and pleasing to God – this is your true and proper worship.
>
> **Romans 12:1**

RESPOND

Think of other Christians in your church/fellowship as fellow team members, with their own tasks and specialisms, complementing and belonging to each other. How might you encourage them?

Bible in a year: Job 5,6; Luke 15

Tuesday 22 July
Romans 12:9–21

What to do and not to do

PREPARE

Pray to be a doer of the Word and not a reader only.

READ

Romans 12:9–21

EXPLORE

This is one of the Bible's most practical passages. It mentions about 21 things to do, and 7 things not to do. Its meaning is mostly straightforward. The hard part is living it out.

Overall, good Christian living is about love (v 9), and, as the passage makes clear, it needs to be a sincere, practical and resilient love. In a loving church, the Christians will have a mutual commitment to, and respect for, each other (v 10). Love will be hard work sometimes: for example, when entertaining visitors or refugees, when helping at a food bank or when there is opposition or suffering. This love needs to develop stamina, if we are to keep keen in the Lord's service, including praying for others. Paul knows what it's like. We need to refuel spiritually and to allow our hope of glory to cheer us up (vs 11–13)!

Love means doing good to our enemies too, never retaliating or seeking revenge (vs 17,19,20). Our response to evil in the world is not to add to it, but to abhor it and replace it with good (vs 9,20,21). We want to be a blessing to everyone, even to those who reject us. Love includes sympathising with people, not being superior, and living at peace with everyone we can (vs 14–16,18).

Love must be sincere. Hate what is evil; cling to what is good.

Romans 12:9

RESPOND

Select two or three imperatives in the passage that you think may be the Lord's word for you to act on in the coming days.

Bible in a year: Job 7,8; Psalms 81,82

Wednesday 23 July

Romans 13:1–7

God's public servants

PREPARE

Resolve that the next few minutes will be a good investment. Make the most of the time, absorbing something of God's Word.

READ

Romans 13:1–7

EXPLORE

'What do you do?' the hitchhiker asked the driver who had stopped to pick him up. 'I'm in public service,' the man replied, with a marked Welsh accent. The driver was the then Speaker of the British House of Commons, George Thomas. 'Public servants' is how we often describe our politicians, police, judges, administrators etc, and so they are. It is a noble calling. In our passage we find that they are not just servants of the public but 'servants of God' (vs 4,6).

God has given them authority to govern, maintain order, administer justice, commend those who do right and punish those who do wrong. God has set this up for the common good (vs 3,4).

In essence, our primary duty as Christian citizens is to subject ourselves (vs 1,5) to these God-given 'governing authorities', so that society can function well. We pay our taxes, even if we don't agree with everything the government does. We show respect to officials, even when we think they're wrong, out of respect for their office (v 7). Ultimately, if governments or officials go badly wrong, other scriptures speak about how to oppose, resist or patiently endure them, like the examples of Daniel, Jesus himself or his apostles.

Give to everyone what you owe them: if you owe taxes, pay taxes; if revenue, then revenue; if respect, then respect; if honour, then honour.

Romans 13:7

RESPOND

Pray for those in prison and for those who have been affected as a consequence: their victims and their families, and the prisoners' partners and children.

Bible in a year: Job 9,10; Luke 16

Action time

PREPARE

'Know yourself' said an ancient oracle. Ask the Lord to show you yourself as well as your Saviour.

READ

Romans 13:8–14

EXPLORE

'Wake up!' The words may mean we have lost concentration, or that it is time to rise and get dressed at the beginning of the day. There is an urgency in Paul's words (vs 11,12). He is reminding the Christians in Rome that a new day has dawned with the resurrection of Jesus and the present old era will pass away without further notice. The trouble is that we believers can blithely carry on as if in a daze, oblivious that our behaviour still reflects the dark old times. 'Change now!' is the message. We need a change of clothes into new behaviour that reflects Jesus Christ (v 14).

So some old behaviour needs to be thrown away: in fact, all the ugly items in verse 13. They are quite out of place in Christ's new world. Then we need to kit ourselves out with some new behaviour – in summary, love for other people. For example, we must choose to respect people's life and property so that we do not steal or kill. We must choose self-control in sexual matters so that we do not commit adultery. We must choose contentment so that we do not covet what belongs to another (v 9). This is the love required (v 10). This is the love Jesus taught (Matthew 19:18,19).

And do this, understanding the present time: the hour has already come for you to wake up from your slumber, because our salvation is nearer now than when we first believed.

Romans 13:11

RESPOND

Do you have a pattern of behaviour that needs changing? Can you think of a strategy for achieving it?

Bible in a year: Job 11,12; Luke 17

Friday 25 July
Romans 14:1–12

Different opinions

PREPARE
Pray to learn something you need from the Lord today.

READ
Romans 14:1–12

EXPLORE
It was over 50 years ago and it seems silly now. I was in a hot, crowded, stuffy church on a sultry Sunday evening. Most men had taken their jackets off (yes, the men were wearing jackets then!) to feel more comfortable. I took my jacket off but felt distinctly uncomfortable. Somehow, I felt I was being disrespectful to God, to the church and to the Lord's Day, worshipping there in my shirtsleeves. So I put my jacket back on and felt at ease again. My friends smiled indulgently at me. (Nowadays, my conscience does not object if I worship dressed more casually.)

How do we react to Christian people whose conscience is more sensitive than others', especially about something we think of as minor? In Paul's day, perhaps some believers could not bring themselves to eat meat that had passed through pagan temple processes. Or perhaps opinions varied about whether observing certain days, eg for prayer or fasting (vs 2,5), was helpful or unhelpful.

Don't think worse of a believer whose conscience is different from yours, says Paul (vs 3,10). Rather, show them respect for wanting the best (v 6). The Lord knows their heart. We must not get above ourselves. Who are we to set ourselves up as judge of someone else's conscience? We and they are all answerable to God (vs 11,12).

If we live, we live for the Lord; and if we die, we die for the Lord. So, whether we live or die, we belong to the Lord.

Romans 14:8

RESPOND
Think of someone you know who has a different opinion from you on some aspect of conscience. Determine not to fall out over it!

Bible in a year: Job 13,14; Luke 18

Saturday 26 July
Romans 14:13–23

Mountains and molehills

PREPARE

As you open today's passage, open your heart both to the Lord and to the needs of others.

READ

Romans 14:13–23

EXPLORE

Seeing things in their right perspective can sometimes be difficult in Christian circles. Big things can get ignored and small things can become huge. In Rome, it may have been the case (though we are not told the details) that some Jewish Christians were still only comfortable eating meat according to the strict Jewish way, and they found it deeply upsetting to their faith that Gentile followers of their Messiah would eat any meat cooked anyhow. Was this a big matter? Yes, to those Jews! But to those Gentiles? No, they carried on regardless.

Paul's view on it (and God's) is different. Something we regard as minor is a major thing if it builds up, or trips up, someone else's faith (vs 13,15). Our molehill can be another person's mountain. What we eat and drink in themselves are clearly not as important as doing right and pursuing peace (v 17). Yet if our choices in these mundane matters affect the exercise of someone's faith and conscience, they can become very significant.

Avoiding, say, a meal once associated with paganism, or a glass of alcohol, because of someone else's weakness or sensibility, may be very constructive and supportive (vs 19,21). Things that build up another's faith and encourage unity are big things.

For the kingdom of God is not a matter of eating and drinking, but of righteousness, peace and joy in the Holy Spirit.

Romans 14:17

RESPOND

How well do you know your conscience? Is it sensitive enough? Or too sensitive? Do you listen to it? Thank God for it.

Bible in a year: Job 15–17; Psalms 83,84

Sunday 27 July

Psalm 48

City view

PREPARE

Like the prodigal son with his father (Luke 15:18–21), let us humble ourselves before our Father in heaven.

READ

Psalm 48

EXPLORE

There are many towns and cities in Europe with ancient walls still standing, testifying to the defence of the town centuries ago. Tourists and locals can walk along the walls and enjoy a fine panorama of the town, absorbing the history of the place.

Jerusalem was similar. People rejoiced to 'walk about Zion' (v 12). Its impressive defences reminded them of the city's past deliverances. They saw the city's great beauty, and more importantly they recalled the city's Great King who had graciously saved them (vs 1,2). From the walls, they could see where, fairly recently, vast Assyrian forces had besieged the city but had then been thoroughly vanquished (vs 4–7). The people had *heard* about the Lord's saving power; now they *looked* at it, in this very place (v 8). The beauty and security of Jerusalem's architecture strengthened everyone's faith in God's power and continuing love (vs 9–11).

They may have walked around Zion physically, or they may have done it in their imagination ('meditation', v 9). We can all view Jerusalem in our mind's eye: see its impressive walls, the towers, the Temple, and then the cross, the empty tomb, and the Pentecost crowd. We too can meditate on this city of the Great King, who will be our God for ever, alongside us to the end (vs 2,14).

For this God is our God for ever and ever; he will be our guide even to the end.

Psalm 48:14

RESPOND

Pray for peace, security and confidence for all people living in present-day Jerusalem.

Bible in a year: Job 18,19; Luke 19

Give way!

PREPARE

A prayer to start with: 'Lord, mould me today as a potter moulds her clay. Amen.'

READ

Romans 15:1–6

EXPLORE

'Give way!' says the road sign, as the traffic lanes merge. Are you the sort of person in life who tends to give way when there's conflict or do you dig in your heels? The truth is, of course, that sometimes we need to be able to stand firm and sometimes we need to be able to give way, or to negotiate. Love 'is not self-seeking,' says the apostle elsewhere (1 Corinthians 13:5). Paul is saying here we need to develop an ability to give way to others ('not to please ourselves', v 1).

The supreme example is so obvious we might miss it – the Lord Jesus himself. His whole ministry and sacrifice could be summed up as not pleasing himself. The Old Testament reinforces this, highlighting for us how he willingly suffered in his Father's service (v 3).

All this is very practical. The Scriptures, as always, give us encouragement to endure (v 4). Jesus' example inspires us to live for the good of others, not just for our own pleasure (v 2). In the church fellowship, there are bound to be some tensions and differences of opinion. But, if everyone shows this same generosity of spirit toward each other that Jesus showed, then our worship and our fellowship will glorify God so much more (vs 5,6).

For even Christ did not please himself.

Romans 15:3a

RESPOND

'The fruit of the Spirit is ... forbearance' (Galatians 5:22). How true is this in your life and experience?

Bible in a year: Job 20,21; Luke 20

Tuesday 29 July
Romans 15:7–13

For the many not the few

PREPARE
Step outside your own life and fellowship for a few minutes to hear the Lord speak to you from his worldwide vantage point.

READ
Romans 15:7–13

EXPLORE
If you're writing a long email, you might want to mention your main points again at the end. As Paul begins to conclude this major letter to the Romans, he underlines the good news that the gospel is for everyone everywhere. He stresses it four times.

1 Christ became a servant for Jew and Gentile alike (vs 8,9). **2** In Christ, God fulfils his promises to the Jews in such a way that non-Jews (Gentiles) also can praise God for his mercy (vs 8–11). **3** From the beginning, God intended the Jews to be his instrument through whom the whole world might come to praise and glorify God (v 12). **4** The exalted Christ reigns in righteousness over all the nations of the world. Because of this, all people can have hope (v 12).

The practical implications for us are, first, to accept one another, as Christ accepted us (v 7). How terrible if we should shun someone for whom Christ died. Secondly, be filled with hope! Think about verse 13. We could learn it by heart. Trust the God of hope. He has worked down the centuries to bring joy and peace in Christ to us, whoever we are, by the power of his Spirit (v 13).

May the God of hope fill you with all joy and peace as you trust in him, so that you may overflow with hope by the power of the Holy Spirit.
Romans 15:13

RESPOND
Think of all the various ways Christians in different countries praise God and bring glory to him. Give thanks to God for this wonderful worldwide spread of the gospel.

Bible in a year: Job 22,23; Psalm 85

Gospel imperatives

PREPARE

Be curious, looking for something in the Bible that is new, unexpected or forgotten, and receive it gladly.

READ

Romans 15:14–22

EXPLORE

Paul was more sensitive and more considerate than he is often given credit for. Was he worried here that he might not have got the tone quite right for his audience? He fulsomely reassured them of his high opinion of them (vs 14,15) and he offered a further explanation (following 1:10–13) for why he had not visited them yet (v 22).

The main reason behind everything Paul did was that God had given him this huge privilege of 'ministering Jesus Christ' to the non-Jewish world (vs 15,16). Three times Paul mentions 'proclaiming the gospel' (vs 16,19,20). This was his over-arching joy, duty and ambition. Hence his delay in visiting Rome. He had been busy! He felt he was primarily a pioneer and therefore should prioritise places where the gospel had not yet reached (v 20).

When I was 21, someone much older implored me, 'When you are a vicar in a new parish, please remember that God was at work there before you.' A strong sense of call to God's work doesn't mean we can ignore God's people around us. See how Paul, the great apostle to the unreached, still affirmed the brave Christians in Rome; he still took trouble to explain his plans to them (v 22) and he took care not to muscle in on someone else's ministry (v 20).

It has always been my ambition to preach the gospel where Christ was not known, so that I would not be building on someone else's foundation.
Romans 15:20

RESPOND

Pray for wisdom to know when to resist other people's expectations and when to accept other people's advice and insight.

Bible in a year: Job 24–26; Luke 21

Thursday 31 July

Romans 15:23–33

Please pray

PREPARE

Pray this Bible reader's prayer: 'Lord, may your Word be my rule, may your Holy Spirit be my teacher and may I be a good learner today. Amen.'

READ

Romans 15:23–33

EXPLORE

Life was never easy for Paul. But he must have been worried about road safety. Bandits were common. He was uninsured, on a long journey, carrying a large amount of cash collected from the churches of Macedonia and Greece to relieve poverty in their 'mother' church in Jerusalem. Was he carrying large bags of gold coins? Sea travel was hazardous too. Paul was shipwrecked four times in all.

Also, if he arrived in Jerusalem safely, he faced an uncertain reception. Jewish opponents might block him or even try to kill him (as did in fact happen, Acts 23:12–22) and Jewish Christians might not accept a gift from Gentile Christians (v 31), or they might not see the importance of believers from different cultures helping each other in a united church (v 17). Moreover, Paul was determined, under God, to go to Spain (another long journey!) and yet he longed to visit the church at Rome for some fellowship and support (vs 23,24,28,32).

So, please pray! he urged (v 30). Even if we are trying to do God's will and are mindful of God's good providence, we still need the prayers of the Christian family, and they need ours.

I urge you, brothers and sisters, by our Lord Jesus Christ and by the love of the Spirit, to join me in my struggle by praying to God for me.

Romans 15:30

RESPOND

Is there a church or Christian organisation that has helped you spiritually in the past that you can now help financially or through prayer, to say thank you?

Bible in a year: Job 27,28; Luke 22

Friday 1 August
Romans 16:1–16

Greet if not meet

PREPARE

Pause to ask the Lord to make clear what he has to say to you from his Word for today.

READ

Romans 16:1–16

EXPLORE

Imagine you are gathering in a house in Rome for fellowship and worship. A certain Phoebe (v 1) has brought this letter from Corinth from the apostle Paul addressed to the group. Then imagine that, as it is read out for the first time, you are one of the believers Paul identifies by name as 'my dear friend' (v 8), or 'a hard worker in the Lord' (v 12) or 'faithful to Christ' (v 10). You'd feel ten feet tall!

Which of the 26 believers mentioned here can you identify with most? The heroic (vs 3,4), the house church member (vs 5,14,15), the tested and persecuted (vs 7,10) or the caring and dependable (v 13b)?

Notice Paul's kindness. He greets people personally, by name. Many are women, most of whom he singles out as deserving recognition. Some are Jews, many are Gentiles; some are longstanding believers, some have typical slave names; and Paul greets them all with affection. He knows the value of these short comments of appreciation and encouragement. In addition, Paul asks if anyone can help Phoebe practically while she is in Rome. He hopes so. She has been a generous helper to Paul and many others back home. Christians help people, of course. Supporting someone who has helped others is doubly appropriate (v 2).

> Greet Andronicus and Junia, my fellow Jews who have been in prison with me. They are outstanding among the apostles, and they were in Christ before I was.
>
> **Romans 16:7**

RESPOND

Who can you acknowledge and encourage today by name?

Bible in a year: Job 29,30; Luke 23

Saturday 2 August

Romans 16:17–27

Practical and sublime

PREPARE

Something to consider: are you as sensitive to the Word of God as you are to the words of your friends?

READ

Romans 16:17–27

EXPLORE

Watch out for scammers, we are told. Such people phone us or email us and they sound genuine but they're not. It's all very convincing. They pressure us to do what they say. But it's a scam. They are trying to steal our money. We need to be alert and hang up.

'Watch out' is Paul's final practical message. Watch out for those who are divisive and obstructive in the fellowship. They may be able to talk convincingly, but they deceive those who are easily swayed. Steer clear of them. By contrast, Paul is glad about his Roman friends. They are well-practised in following good teaching and have little experience of evil. Paul wants them to keep it that way (vs 17–19).

Paul makes room for sending greetings to Rome from the believers who are gathered around him in Corinth (vs 21–23) before his momentous journey to Jerusalem (Acts 20–26). The end of the letter (vs 25,26) echoes the beginning (1:1–5), reminding us of our debt to Paul for the sublime truths that he laboured to bring us – the good news of Jesus Christ, the eternal purposes of God, the revelation of the Scriptures and the obedience of faith for all peoples. May we be immovable, firmly 'established' (v 25) on these truths.

> The God of peace will soon crush Satan under your feet. The grace of our Lord Jesus be with you.
>
> **Romans 16:20**

RESPOND

Erastus (v 23) was a Christian with considerable civic responsibility in Corinth. Pray for those who work in government locally in your city, town or district.

Bible in a year: Job 31,32; Psalms 86,87

Sunday 3 August
Psalm 49

God, death and wealth

PREPARE

'Hear' and 'listen' to gain 'wisdom' and 'understanding', says today's psalm (vs 1–3). Pray that you may do just that.

READ

Psalm 49

EXPLORE

Money can buy many good things in life. Multimillionaires can buy themselves a tourist ride in space if they wish. Many wealthy (and not so wealthy) people give generously to good causes. Some on the Rich List even pledge to give away their vast fortune during their lifetime.

Money has its limitations too, as all the world can see (vs 1,2). 'You can't take it with you' (v 17). In the end, everyone without exception leaves their money behind (v 10). Beyond the grave, it has no leverage or purchasing power. It cannot buy us a ticket out of death (vs 8,9). In life, money can fund houses and great estates, but the best accommodation it can manage in death is a tomb (v 11)! Yet some still live for their wealth, and in some hands it means oppression and misery for others (vs 5,6).

But what money can't do, God can. 'God will redeem me from … the dead', says our psalmist (v 15). Death is a cash-free zone. But, as the New Testament insists, we are redeemed from futility not with silver and gold but with the precious blood of Christ (1 Peter 1:18,19). Our money will not welcome us into glory, but our Redeemer will (v 15).

But God will redeem me from the realm of the dead; he will surely take me to himself.
Psalm 49:15

RESPOND

Money and death affect us all. Pray for help and support for those with money issues and for those attending the funeral of a loved one at this time.

Bible in a year: Job 33,34; Luke 24

Genesis 28–35

Presence and promise

About the writer
John Grayston

Now retired after 37 years serving in various roles on Scripture Union staff, John is part of the teaching team in his church and also teaches regularly in other churches and on Oak Hall holidays. He and his wife Jenny have two children and seven grandchildren. He prefers walking in the mountains or cultivating his allotment to sitting on the beach.

For the next two weeks we will be joining Jacob as he runs from his brother Esau and then later returns. It's not always easy to like Jacob. In earlier readings we have seen how he first stole Esau's birthright and then his blessing. He is devious, deceptive and manipulative – qualities which we shall see repeated as he spends years with his uncle Laban, marries, has children and then finally returns to face Esau.

It is not all bad; he worships God, trusts God (some of the time) and acknowledges God's place in his life. Despite his flawed character and inconsistent behaviour, God meets with him again and again, in his grace ever-present. Jacob is still within the promise and purpose of God to bless all nations through Abraham's descendants (Genesis 12:1–3).

We who fail frequently can be encouraged. God does not give up on us. His promise to us is different from the promise to Jacob and we live in a very different world. But he has assured us that he will never leave us (Hebrews 13:5). That does not give us permission to behave as we like, but it does reassure us that when we fail and return we will be received. God is still working out his ultimate purpose to restore all things through Jesus. As you read, look for places where you see God at work today, in your life, in your church and in the wider world.

Monday 4 August

Genesis 28:10–22

God never lets go

PREPARE

Sit quietly and expectantly, looking for God to come and meet with you. Sense his presence, awesome and mysterious, gracious and loving.

READ

Genesis 28:10–22

EXPLORE

Jacob is heading for Harran for two reasons: first, Esau is out for revenge for his stolen inheritance and blessing; and secondly, his mother Rebekah has ensured that Isaac, his father, sends him off with a blessing to find a wife from her own people. So this is not a happy journey. His life may not be falling apart, but it is fraught. Then God steps into the picture and reminds him of his promise to Abraham, a promise which now involves Jacob. Note how similar the language is to Genesis 13, verses 14 and 15. Jacob responds with awe, worship and obedience.

When we have questions, doubts and fears, when life is not working out as hoped, we may need to remind ourselves of God's presence and promise. It is not that God has left us, although it may feel like it. He has not forgotten his promise. Sometimes we will have powerful experiences of God being with us, sometimes a quiet assurance, and sometimes we just have to hold on to his promise. He will faithfully ensure that the plans he has for us will come to completion. We can journey on confidently, despite the pressures and the fears.

He was afraid and said, 'How awesome is this place! This is none other than the house of God; this is the gate of heaven.'

Genesis 28:17

RESPOND

Recall a special time of meeting with God. How did it make you feel? What impact does it have on your life today? How might you draw fresh confidence and direction from it?

Bible in a year: Job 35,36; Philippians 1

Tuesday 5 August
Genesis 29:1–14a

God in the everyday

PREPARE

Open your heart and mind to the God who meets us in the everyday. Prepare to meet him in the ordinariness of today.

READ

Genesis 29:1–14a

EXPLORE

Sometimes we have great spiritual experiences – it may be at a large celebration, in our regular Bible reading, in a conversation with a friend or as we reflect on the wonders of creation. But most of life is not like that. It is more ordinary and sometimes it is hard to see where God is or what he is doing. Jacob would have identified with that. Yesterday, we read about Jacob's awesome and powerful meeting with God. Today he is back to the world of long journeys and meetings. His Bethel moment is replaced by a getting-water-for-sheep moment, the spectacular by the mundane. But this meeting with Rachel is a key part of the narrative, moving God's story forward.

While it may not be so obvious that God is still leading him, his presence is just as real, if not as spectacular. So it is with us. God is with us in everyday encounters in the workplace, at the school gates, on social media, in the coffee shop. For Jacob, what appear to be chance encounters are part of God's plan to fulfil his promise to Abraham. For us, apparently chance encounters may be God-appointed moments to show and share his love.

When Jacob saw Rachel daughter of his uncle Laban, and Laban's sheep, he went over and rolled the stone away from the mouth of the well and watered his uncle's sheep.

Genesis 29:10

RESPOND

Pray about some of the encounters you will have this week. How might you see them as opportunities to experience God's presence and to show his love?

Bible in a year: Job 37,38; Psalm 88

Wednesday 6 August

Genesis 29:14b–30

Unexpected bride

PREPARE

Pray: 'Lord, I release to you any pressure or tension I feel. I calm my busy mind to hear your word to me.'

READ

Genesis 29:14b–30

EXPLORE

This messy story of deceit, sexual desire, exploitation and betrayal does not make for easy reading. The idea of women being used as bargaining pieces is deeply disturbing. Jacob's virtual slavery makes us uncomfortable. But despite significant cultural differences, this is a world we know. Misogyny and objectifying of women are still with us. Slavery can still be found in various forms. Most of us will have experienced exploitation or betrayal in some form or another.

This incident reminds us that life in a broken world populated by fallen human beings will always be messy. But this was never God's intention. He created men and women to be companions sharing together in caring for his creation. Jesus and Paul give new dignity and status to women. In the new community of God's people there is neither slave nor free (Galatians 3:28), preparing the way for the eventual abolition of slavery, admittedly not yet fully achieved. In contrast to a world of lies and manipulation, Jesus models truth and integrity.

Above all, through the mess of today's reading, God is working out his promise to Abraham, and remains faithfully active in the confusion of our individual lives and the brokenness of our world.

When morning came, there was Leah! So Jacob said to Laban, 'What is this you have done to me? I served you for Rachel, didn't I? Why have you deceived me?'

Genesis 29:25

RESPOND

Can you think of anyone caught up in a web of lies and manipulation? Pray for them now.

Bible in a year: Job 39,40; Philippians 2

Thursday 7 August
Genesis 29:31 – 30:24

Happy families?

PREPARE

Take the psalmist's words to heart: 'I have calmed and quietened myself, I am like a weaned child with its mother' (Psalm 131:2).

READ

Genesis 29:31 – 30:24

EXPLORE

This could so easily be the plot of a twenty-first-century soap. Leah lives with the pain of being unloved, Rachel with the pain of childlessness. Jacob enjoys sexual activity without offering genuine affection. He shows little understanding of Rachel's or Leah's pain. And we can only guess at the feelings of Bilhah and Zilpah. This is dysfunctional family life at its worst.

But it is not beyond redemption. The beautiful words 'God remembered Rachel' do not mean that he had forgotten her. They mean that at this point in the story God chose to intervene and show grace to Rachel. Why then and not earlier we cannot know: there are things we do not understand about how God works and sometimes we have to trust without knowing all the answers. The names of all these sons are familiar to us as the tribes of later Israel. We begin to see that the promise to Abraham is for the long term. The mention of Judah brings to mind one who will be known as the 'Lion of the tribe of Judah' (Revelation 5:5). We can rejoice that, out of the pain and difficulty that we see here, Jesus will come to deal with the sin, deceit and failure of humanity, to stand with the lonely, the hurting and the marginalised.

> Then God remembered Rachel; he listened to her and enabled her to conceive.
>
> **Genesis 30:22**

RESPOND

Think of someone you know who is wondering what God is doing. Pray that God will 'remember' them.

Bible in a year: Job 41,42; Philippians 3

Friday 8 August

Genesis 31:1–21

Consequences

PREPARE

Pray these lyrics: 'Speak, Lord, in the stillness,/ while I wait on thee,/ Hushed my heart listen/ In expectancy.'*

READ

Genesis 31:1–21

EXPLORE

Laban is still in the business of deception and manipulation – for some background to these verses, read chapter 30, verses 25–43. With our modern understanding of genetics, these breeding arrangements don't make sense, but God is overruling and frustrating the ploys of Laban and enabling Jacob to prosper. Jacob has the wisdom to recognise this. To believe that we have achieved things in our own strength or through our own ability is a dangerous mistake (Deuteronomy 8:17,18).

Jacob knows that his wealth comes from God and that God is working in his life, but he does not act as if that were true. He has already spoken of his desire to go home (Genesis 30:25) and now, having heard God's instruction, he obeys, but in deceptive ways that will lead to further problems. We too can be tempted to take things into our own hands. The better way is to remember God's past faithfulness and trust him for the future. That does not mean doing nothing; it does mean listening to God and acting in line with what he says.

Rachel and Leah clearly resent the way they have been treated. Laban, through his selfishness, is about to lose his daughters and grandchildren, a direct consequence of his actions. Little we do is done in isolation; there are always consequences.

> Then the LORD said to Jacob, 'Go back to the land of your fathers and to your relatives, and I will be with you.'
>
> **Genesis 31:3**

RESPOND

Pray that you may always be ready to hear God and to obey.

*'Speak, Lord, in the Stillness', Emily Crawford, 1864–1927

Bible in a year: Proverbs 1,2; Philippians 4

Religious smorgasbord

PREPARE

Pray: 'Lord, I come conscious of my failure. Speak your words of forgiveness and comfort to me.'

READ

Genesis 31:22–42

EXPLORE

No one comes out of this well. There is anger, resentment, deception (again!), fear, self-justification and suspicion. Jacob no doubt felt that leaving secretly was the only option, and with good reason given Laban's track record – even here his words about giving them a good send-off ring hollow. Laban does not share Jacob's relationship with God; he talks about the God of *your* father and seems more concerned about the loss of his household gods than anything else, but at least he hears from God and obeys. Rachel seems confused. Was she stealing the household gods to ensure good fortune or to spite her father? Jacob shows faith – but only sometimes and only in part.

We know the feeling. We can get it right, but we can also get it wrong. Sometimes our faith is strong; at other times we fail to trust, we go our own way or we put our trust in the wrong things – not small, man-made statues, but wealth, health, career, relationships... And in a world of many pressures there is always the danger of compromise. Like Rachel, we can absorb the values of surrounding culture in subtle and unnoticed ways. But we have resources that were not available to Jacob – the example of Jesus and the power of the Holy Spirit living in us.

> Then God came to Laban the Aramean in a dream at night and said to him, 'Be careful not to say anything to Jacob, either good or bad.'
>
> **Genesis 31:24**

RESPOND

Pray that you may see clearly when you are in danger of living by the values of your peers rather than the values of Jesus.

Bible in a year: Proverbs 3,4; Psalm 89

Sunday 10 August

Psalm 50

True worship

PREPARE

Today, join the psalmist and prepare to 'Worship the Lord in the splendour of his holiness...' (Psalm 96:9).

READ

Psalm 50

EXPLORE

Today we join with others in worship. It will take different forms. At its best it will be focused on God's character, his saving activity and his purposes in the world. But sometimes it will reflect more of our preferences and desires and be aimed to please us rather than God. This psalm addresses just such issues.

In verses 1–5, God summons his people to the place of judgement. The picture is of a glorious and powerful God, somewhat reminiscent of his appearance at Sinai. Then in verses 6–15, God tells them that, while there is nothing necessarily wrong with their sacrifices, it is their motivation that matters. He does not need their sacrifices, for anything they can offer is already his, but delights in their worship – and ours – if it expresses gratitude (v 14) and dependence (v 15). Worship which, like that of the Pharisee in Jesus' parable (Luke 18:9–14), is more about how well we are doing than about God is not acceptable. Verses 16–23 are darker and touch on the hypocrisy of worship offered to God from those whose lives do not honour him – a reminder that worship is not just about what we do in church on Sunday, but about how we live during the rest of the week.

Sacrifice thank-offerings to God, fulfil your vows to the Most High.

Psalm 50:14

RESPOND

Teach me, my God and King,/ In all things Thee to see,/ And what I do in anything/ To do it as for Thee.*

*George Herbert, 'The Elixir', 1593–1633

Bible in a year: Proverbs 5,6; Colossians 1

Monday 11 August
Genesis 31:43–55

Peace treaty

PREPARE

Recognise that God is an ever-present reality in your life. Sit quietly and allow yourself to become aware of his presence with you now.

READ

Genesis 31:43–55

EXPLORE

How do we settle our differences, especially when there is suspicion and mistrust? Perhaps we don't bother and just let things drift on. Jacob and Laban are determined to have clarity. So they make a covenant, a binding agreement. Today we might have solicitors draw up a document to remind us and to ensure that there will be no misunderstanding later. Their equivalent is a pillar and a heap of stones, acting as a permanent reminder and making the boundaries very clear. Then they have a meal, because that is how in their world you ratify an agreement (v 54). If there are things you need to resolve with others, why not make a plan to do it?

God is the ultimate witness (v 42) who sees all that they do (v 49). God is the final judge who will hold both parties to account (v 53). There is a sacrifice acknowledging that everything has taken place in the presence of God (v 54).

No doubt there were times when Jacob wondered what God was doing, but he never completely lost sight of God who had been ever-present, leading, directing, sustaining, protecting, providing. This is no less true for us. How far are we aware of it?

'Come now, let's make a covenant, you and I, and let it serve as a witness between us.'
Genesis 31:44

RESPOND

Pray that throughout this week you will know that God is with you in every situation. Pray that others will see it and take note.

Bible in a year: Proverbs 7,8; Colossians 2

Tuesday 12 August

Genesis 32:1–21

Trust the promise

PREPARE

Identify some areas of your life in which you want to see God work. Look for his reassurance today.

READ

Genesis 32:1–21

EXPLORE

Laban returns home and Jacob is left to continue his journey with the uncertainty and fear of meeting Esau. If he ever needed reassurance, it is now. And God provides it in the form of a meeting with angels. But this does not completely remove his fear. And so he turns to God with a memorable prayer.

He acknowledges his own weakness. He recognises all that God has done for him. He reminds God of his promises. He prays for protection. There is much that we could learn about prayer from his example. Our prayers are first and foremost to be based on the character and promise of God. They are to be grounded in our relationship with him. They will acknowledge that we are dependent on him. If you have a few moments check these points against the Lord's Prayer in Matthew 6:9–13.

Jacob doesn't seem to have complete confidence in God. Fear makes us behave in strange ways and can work against trust. Jacob carries on with his elaborate plan to pacify Esau with gifts and to protect at least part of his wealth and family by dividing them into two groups (v 7). There's nothing wrong with making plans – unless they reveal a lack of trust in God.

But you have said, 'I will surely make you prosper and will make your descendants like the sand of the sea, which cannot be counted.'

Genesis 32:12

RESPOND

Where do you need to have more faith? Talk to God about it now.

Bible in a year: Proverbs 9,10; Psalm 90

Wednesday 13 August
Genesis 32:22–32

New name, new calling

PREPARE

Almighty God, fill my heart with love for you, my mind with thoughts of you and align my will to yours.

READ

Genesis 32:22–32

EXPLORE

If you are anything like me, you will find this a strange or even disturbing incident. It's not easy to make sense of the details and we wonder what is going on and why it takes place. God initiates the contact/contest for he has new things to teach Jacob. These unexpected meetings with God form a pattern in the life of Jacob. Sometimes God meets us at the times we least expect and in surprising ways. God is not predictable and does not operate in ways that we can understand. But all he does, however strange it may seem, is done for our ultimate benefit.

Names are significant in the ancient world and carry significance and power. Abram becomes Abraham (which is seen as signifying 'father of many nations', Genesis 17:1–8), and now Jacob is renamed Israel. The name change and the blessing are marks of God's call. The change of name sets the tone for the future of God's people. Something significant has happened and life for Jacob will never be quite the same again.

When God calls us to some particular task, he is unlikely to change our names, but he will give us his blessing and the resources that we need. Like Jacob, we may find that life takes on a new dimension.

Then the man said, 'Your name will no longer be Jacob, but Israel, because you have struggled with God and with humans and have overcome.'

Genesis 32:28

RESPOND

Prepare to set out on the next stage of your journey with God with a sense of joy and expectation.

Bible in a year: Proverbs 11,12; Colossians 3

Thursday 14 August

Genesis 33:1–20

Faith sees beyond

PREPARE

Name anything which might distract you. Ask God to help you gather your scattered thoughts and focus on him.

READ

Genesis 33:1–20

EXPLORE

Life can be confusing. Sometimes it is hard to make sense of things and decide on the best course of action. Take comfort from Jacob. On the one hand, he is still suspicious, possibly with good reason, devious, deceptive and perhaps self-serving. On the other he has a sense of guilt, wants reconciliation with Esau and is prepared to make reparation for his previous behaviour, although it does look a little like a bribe. He acknowledges that God has provided for him (v 5).

God remains at the centre of his life. The exact meaning of 'El Elohe Israel' (v 20) is uncertain, but it firmly links Jacob/Israel with God. His use of his new name highlights his acceptance of his new calling and relationship with God. His building of an altar indicates to us that, although Jacob only owns a small portion of the land, he has faith for more. It reminds us of Abraham, who travelled through the land, promised but not yet owned, erecting altars as a mark of faith (12:7,8; 13:4,18). Both men are mentioned in Hebrews 11 as examples of faith. Against the odds, they believed that God would be true to his promise and come through. Having faith and being in God's plan does not require perfection. And that gives us hope.

For a hundred pieces of silver, he bought from the sons of Hamor, the father of Shechem, the plot of ground where he pitched his tent. There he set up an altar and called it El Elohe Israel.

Genesis 33:19,20

RESPOND

Where might you need to exercise more faith in the promises of God? Pray that God will increase your faith and confidence in him.

Bible in a year: Proverbs 13,14; Colossians 4

Friday 15 August
Genesis 35:1–15

Back to the beginning

PREPARE

Recall your first experience of God. Let that memory prepare you to meet with him in new ways today.

READ

Genesis 35:1–15

EXPLORE

We can be slow to learn. Lessons have to be repeated. God takes Jacob back to where it all started. Sometimes going back is the best way forward. If we lose sight of God, we can remind ourselves of the time God first met with us and let that strengthen our faith. When doubts and questions arise, we can go back to the cross of Jesus and recall his love.

Going back gives us an opportunity to refocus our priorities. It will help us to get rid of anything which might pull us away. Far from the household gods providing protection, they have proved a hindrance. It's good to review from time to time and get rid of anything that is hindering or damaging our relationship with God.

Once Jacob has refocused, he is in a better position to hear God refresh his promise and renew his call with a further reminder of his new name. God has great things for him. They are not dependent on Jacob – although he has to play his part of worship and obedience – but on the faithfulness and the long-term plan of God. Today we, the church of Jesus Christ, have a role to play in God's faithful plan for his world.

And God said to him, 'I am God Almighty; be fruitful and increase in number. A nation and a community of nations will come from you, and kings will be among your descendants.'

Genesis 35:11

RESPOND

What might you need to put aside in order to give God his rightful place in your life?

Bible in a year: Proverbs 15,16; 1 Thessalonians 1

Saturday 16 August

Genesis 35:16–29

Blessing for the nations

PREPARE

Invite God to renew his call on your life.

READ

Genesis 35:16–29

EXPLORE

Here's a glimpse into the future. We have met these names before and have noted that they will become familiar as the tribes of Israel who will later enter the Promised Land and from whom will come the Saviour not just of Israel but of the whole world. (It's worth noting that when the land is divided, Levi, having become the priestly tribe, has no land allotted while Joseph's sons Ephraim and Manasseh both receive land.) The promise to Abraham, renewed to Jacob, is fulfilled in the people of Israel but receives its ultimate fulfilment in Jesus (Galatians 3:16), through whose death and resurrection the whole world is blessed.

There is pain. Rachel the beloved wife dies. Benjamin has a special place in his father's heart – Jacob too readily has favourites, an attitude which leads to trouble (37:4). Reuben has sex with Bilhah – an action which will have far-reaching consequences (49:3,4).

Isaac dies, but his death brings about a further reconciliation between Jacob and Esau. The brokenness of the world is evident.

We are invited to see our place in God's ongoing plan for the world. Although separated from Jacob by hundreds of years, we stand in the same purpose of God – to redeem fallen humanity, restore a broken world and form a new community of people who will bear witness to his deeds.

Isaac ... died and was gathered to his people, old and full of years. And his sons Esau and Jacob buried him.

Genesis 35:28,29

RESPOND

Thank God that in Jesus, he is making all things new. Ask what you can do to share this good news.

Bible in a year: Proverbs 17,18; Psalm 91

Sunday 17 August
Psalm 51:1–19

Forgiven praise

PREPARE

'Ransomed, healed, restored, forgiven,/ Who like thee his praise should sing?'*

READ

Psalm 51:1–19

EXPLORE

David knows he has messed up. Probably not surprising, as a prophet has told him a story about a rich man robbing a poor man of his lamb, and when David becomes angry at the rich man's behaviour hits him with, 'You are the man!' (2 Samuel 12:7). Harder for us in a world of compromised standards where knowing right and wrong can be difficult and where we can be subtly affected by the worldview and moral standards of those around. It's worth making a regular practice of asking God to show you where you have gone wrong, and perhaps find a 'prophet', a trusted friend to whom you can be accountable.

Overwhelmed by the enormity of his failure, David turns to God, confesses his sin and pleads for forgiveness and restoration (vs 7–12). He knows he deserves nothing, but that God is gracious – something which we can see even more clearly as a result of Jesus' death. This is where we often leave this psalm, but there is more. David promises, once forgiven and restored, to praise God (v 14) and tell others how good God is (vs 13,15). That's an important part of his story and of ours. Forgiveness is not just for our personal benefit, something to keep to ourselves; it is good news to tell.

Deliver me from the guilt of bloodshed, O God, you who are God my Saviour, and my tongue will sing of your righteousness.

Psalm 51:14

RESPOND

Think about the way that God has forgiven you and praise him. Who could you tell about it this week?

*'Praise, My Soul, the King of Heaven', Henry Francis Lyte, 1793–1847

Bible in a year: Proverbs 19,20; 1 Thessalonians 2

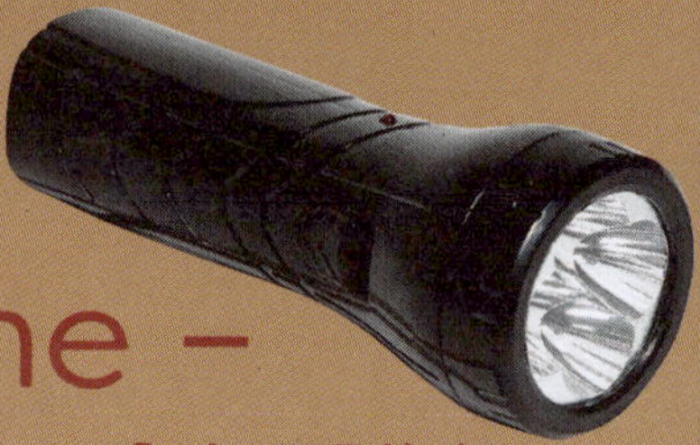

The Bible and me –

a ministry trainer's experience of the Bible

In this Spotlight article, we asked a youth ministry educator and trainer to tell us a little about what the Bible means to him. **Graham Stanton** is ordained in the Anglican Church of Australia and is a member of St Jude's in Parkville, Melbourne.

What was your first Bible?

I've owned my own Bible at least from as early as 8 years old. I know this because I still have my copy of the 1971 hardcover edition of the RSV Bible. The details on the presentation page are in my own handwriting: 'Presented to Graham by Mummy and Daddy, 9.10.76.' I'm loath to count how many Bibles I've owned since then, for fear that I may have owned more copies than times that I've read it through.

Why have you continued to read the Bible?

My daily reading practice still goes through seasons of greater and lesser consistency. Here are three of my favourite quotations about the Bible that keep me coming back to continue, or renew, or recapture my routines:

'The splendour of the divine countenance ... is for us like an inextricable labyrinth unless we are conducted into it by the thread of the word; so that it is better to limp along this path than to dash with all speed outside it.'

This quotation comes from the sixteenth-century reformation leader John Calvin, in the *Institutes of the Christian Religion* (1.6.3). I love his description of the reason that we read the Bible in the first place: that we might behold something of 'the splendour of the divine countenance'. Or, in simpler language, to see God's face and be wowed by it! What a gift we have in the Bible that gives us 'the light of the knowledge of God's glory displayed in the face of Christ' (2 Corinthians 4:6).

Calvin reminds us that the Bible is indeed a precious gift, because without it we'd be lost in an 'inextricable labyrinth'. That is, we'd be stuck, with no way of finding a way through on our own. But the Word leads us forward, even if at times we find it difficult to understand what we're reading. It may be slow-going, but better to shuffle down the right track than to run in the wrong direction.

That idea of sticking at reading the Bible even when it's hard is what the second quote is about. It's from theologian Miroslav Volf, in his book *Captive to the Word*, which says, 'In our encounter with the Bible, tarrying in persistent non-understanding is often the condition of possibility of genuine disclosure, in which we hear more than just the echo of our own internal voice' (2010, p35).

'Tarrying in persistent non-understanding' is such a beautiful way of saying sticking with the Bible even when what I'm reading still doesn't make sense. I don't read the Bible once and have all its mysteries revealed. The Bible isn't like a newspaper article to be read and consumed like a fast-food meal. I read the Bible over and over and over again, in faith that God will keep his promise: that by reading these words we might 'hear his voice' (Hebrews 3:7). We read the Bible because we trust that, as we keep listening, we will hear a revelation from God that speaks something new into our lives.

Finally, the third quote, and my favourite of all, is from the Anglican Prayer book. After the Bible reading in church, the reader says, 'This is the Word of the Lord', and the congregation responds with 'Thanks be to God'. Thanks be to God indeed! We've just been given the opportunity to pay attention to scripture 'as to a light shining in a dark place' (2 Peter 1:19). The liturgy reminds me that reading the Bible and hearing it read is a gift of grace. God didn't have to speak to us, but he has! Many people don't have the privilege of hearing the Scriptures read in their own language, but we have! So it's good and right that our first response is one of thanks.

I especially like the way that the Anglican liturgy invites us to give thanks to God even before we've had the Word explained to us. I'm very thankful for preachers and teachers (and *Daily Bread* note-writers!), who, like Timothy, are able to correctly handle the word of truth (see 2 Timothy 2:15). But before preachers and teachers can do their work of teaching the Bible, we should give thanks that we have the Bible in the first place.

Reading the Bible is not always easy, but it's always worth it. And for that, I am deeply thankful.

Graham Stanton

WAY IN

Acts 16:11 – 20:38

Turned upside down

Let's head into an adventure together. The Acts of the Apostles could be known as the Acts of the Holy Spirit – turning the world upside down. Or the right way up! As we read about the missionary journeys of Paul and his companions, we'll travel through Asia Minor, now modern-day Turkey, and discover how the good news of Jesus began to spread, giving rise to Turkey being called the 'Second Holy Land', the cradle of the young Christian church. Just before writing this, I was privileged to lead a pilgrimage to visit many of the places mentioned, and the Christian heritage is still visible, although many ancient churches are being turned into mosques. Turkey needs our prayers.

Paul was born in Tarsus, in modern-day Turkey. On these journeys we will be reading about, he travelled vast distances, presumably walking, as the Spirit led him on to the next place, the next adventure, the next preaching of the good news of Jesus. From Acts 13 on, it's really the Acts of Paul, directed and empowered by the Spirit, as he interacts with men and women, wealthy and poor, Gentiles and Jews. Even more, it's the Acts of the Spirit, with energy and excitement, crises and persecution. A microcosm of the present-world church. How will it inspire our lives and ministry today?

You might like to find a map of Paul's journeys – either online or at the back of a Bible – to see exactly where we'll be.

About the writer
Penelope Swithinbank

Penelope is ordained in the Anglican Church and is a Chaplain at Bath Abbey. She has written three books, led many pilgrimages and has offered Spiritual Accompaniment for many years. Penelope is married to Kim, who is also ordained in the Anglican Church, and they have three adult children and six grandchildren. Her other passions include books, sunshine, dogs, travel and the theatre. They live in Combe Down, Bath and attend Holy Trinity Church.

An influencer

PREPARE

Prayerfully ask the Lord to bring to your mind those who have influenced you in your faith journey. Thank him for them.

READ

Acts 16:11–15

EXPLORE

Are you on social media? Do you follow any influencers or fashion designers? Lydia was in that world, trading in the most expensive purple cloth; a person of means, an entrepreneur, able to have her own household (vs 14,15) with room for hospitality. She was from Thyatira, an important centre of the cloth trade, and had already become a worshipper of God.

Maybe Lydia was also an influencer. Paul later wrote a very personal letter to the Philippian church, full of joy; and a church grew in Thyatira too (Revelation 2:18). Did Lydia take the message home with her on a visit? We don't know for certain, but from this little group of women the gospel undoubtedly spread.

Where do you interact with others? For instance, social media, work, school, the gym, travelling, commuting or shopping? You may not be either an influencer or an entrepreneur, but, like Lydia, we each have people and places in our lives where we can be an influencer in the power of the Holy Spirit. How might the Lord be calling you to be an influencer, talking about his good news to others?

> When she and the members of her household were baptised, she invited us to her home. 'If you consider me a believer in the Lord,' she said, 'come and stay at my house.' And she persuaded us.
>
> **Acts 16:15**

RESPOND

Lydia devoted herself to the Lord (v 15). Ask the Holy Spirit to help you be an influencer and to refresh your vision and calling as you devote yourself to the Lord and to his good news.

Bible in a year: Proverbs 21,22; 1 Thessalonians 3

Tuesday 19 August

Acts 16:16–28

In the name of Jesus!

PREPARE

Hold out open hands to God, as a symbol of willingness for whatever he wants in your life.

READ

Acts 16:16–28

EXPLORE

Did you notice the brief sentence Paul uses to heal the young slave girl? 'In the name of Jesus Christ I *command* you to come out of her!' (v 18, italics mine). There's no laying hands on her or anointing with oil (not that there's anything wrong with those: James 5:14) nor a lengthy prayer. It's short, simple, sincere. And authoritative. Not, 'If it's your will, please heal her.' Is it a bit of a cop-out if we pray like that? Or a good excuse if nothing happens?

Two things stand out for me in these verses. First, Paul doesn't hesitate: he loudly prays a quick, commanding, healing prayer on the spot. I remember John Wimber saying how they used to pray for no one and no one was healed; and then they prayed for everyone and some were healed, and at least it was an improvement.

Secondly, the girl was a slave, used by her owners as an oracle or medium. There are many enslaved people today, apparently more than ever before. We can't change history, but we can change how we react to such issues today. We can make a difference for the lives of enslaved adults and children, just as Paul tried to (and was thrown into prison with Silas for doing so).

She followed Paul and the rest of us, shouting, 'These men are servants of the Most High God, who are telling you the way to be saved.'

Acts 16:17

RESPOND

Who do you know who needs healing prayer? What could you do to help end slavery? Ask for the Spirit's guidance as you think about these questions.

Bible in a year: Proverbs 23,24; Psalms 92,93

Wednesday 20 August
Acts 16:29–40

From prison to praise

PREPARE

Listen to, and/or sing aloud, a praise and worship song or hymn. Take a moment to think of the one you'd like to use.

READ

Acts 16:29–40

EXPLORE

Did Paul and Silas wonder where it all went wrong, or why they'd been diverted to Philippi? And yet, even in prison, they were still praying and singing and worshipping God! The Spirit hadn't left them – Paul could sense what the jailer was about to do. (He couldn't see; there were no lights, v 29.) The terrified jailer, fearing at least torture if not death if prisoners escaped, cried out, 'How do I get out of this mess?'

Is it a deeply theological question? He knew nothing, or next to nothing, about Christian faith and belief. But Paul and Silas knew the deep answer, if you look at their reply. None of them went to bed that night; there was a heart-to-heart about the gospel, and lots of baptising; the jailer gave them medical attention and a meal, and then... Then there was yet more rejoicing (v 34). How do you think Paul and Silas felt at that point?

What influence did the prayer and praising have? Think about it in regard to the Holy Spirit, the prisoners, the jailer and the situation. It's certainly a powerful reminder to 'give thanks in all circumstances' (1 Thessalonians 5:18).

The jailer brought them into his house and set a meal before them; he was filled with joy because he had come to believe in God – he and his whole household.

Acts 16:34

RESPOND

What are the differences between praise, worship and thanksgiving? What difference do praise and worship make in your life? How could you praise God more – now and every day?

Bible in a year: Proverbs 25,26; 1 Thessalonians 4

Thursday 21 August

Acts 17:1–15

Is it worth it?

PREPARE

Thank Jesus that he never changes: he is the same, yesterday, today and for ever. Recall some of his characteristics you particularly appreciate.

READ

Acts 17:1–15

EXPLORE

How do you feel when change looms? Psychologists say that fear of change, metathesiophobia, is one of the biggest fears affecting people's lives and it can paralyse and impede anyone. Change can indeed be scary; we prefer to remain within our comfort zones. Yet anything that doesn't change becomes static or may even die.

So maybe we can sympathise with the rioters in these verses, to some extent. They didn't want anything to change; they believed in the rightness of their beliefs and were not persuaded by Paul's message. They were jealous of the attention Paul was getting and his influence on others. They were jealous and they were fearful, and they incited a riot. And so the pattern continues. Paul preaches, there is huge opposition often leading to imprisonment and torture, or Paul and his companions have to escape (vs 10,13).

Dr Helen Roseveare, a Christian missionary who was tortured for her faith in the Congo in the twentieth century, was asked if it was worth it. No, she replied, but he is worthy.

'They are all defying Caesar's decrees, saying that there is another king, one called Jesus.'

Acts 17:7

RESPOND

What would you do if you faced huge change in your life, especially if it involved opposition to your faith? Is it worth it? Pray for persecuted Christians around the world.

Bible in a year: Proverbs 27,28; 1 Thessalonians 5

Friday 22 August
Acts 17:16–34

Speaking words of wisdom

PREPARE

Who do you know who needs to hear the good news of Jesus?

READ

Acts 17:16–34

EXPLORE

While Paul waits in Athens, he engages in the Athenian pursuit of debating. After wandering around sightseeing, he gets involved with the Epicureans, who thought life was 'eat, drink and be merry' and the Stoics, who believed it was better to live simply, practise self-discipline and be indifferent to pleasure and pain. Both sides agreed they wanted to hear more about Paul's ideas and took him to the Areopagus to speak to judges, councillors and philosophers.

Isn't it interesting how different Paul's speech in Athens is to how he has preached before? Here, although distressed by altars seen in the city, he immediately looks for ways to connect with the locals. He mentions what is common to them all and then speaks to the culture of their day. He mentions their great interest in spirituality, in creation and the environment, then he cleverly links it all to the good news of Jesus.

What similarities can you spot with our own culture in the twenty-first century?

Jesus promised that the Holy Spirit would give words to his disciples at a time of challenge. 'The Holy Spirit will give you the right words when the time comes' (Luke 12:12, *The Message*), and we can expect the same. When and where might you be needing 'the right words'?

> '... I even found an altar with this inscription: TO AN UNKNOWN GOD. So you are ignorant of the very thing you worship – and this is what I am going to proclaim to you.'
>
> **Acts 17:23**

RESPOND

As you pray for someone needing to hear the good news, ask for the right words at the right time.

Bible in a year: Proverbs 29,30; 2 Thessalonians 1

Saturday 23 August

Acts 18:1–17

Guidance

PREPARE

Ask God to speak to you through today's verses. Tell him you want to be open to the Word, the healing, the probing, the consolation, the guidance – whatever you need. And ask for grace to accept it.

READ

Acts 18:1–17

EXPLORE

Do you find it difficult to know God's guidance? Or find it comes at the last minute? Or worry that you'll miss God's plans? It's interesting how the Lord guided Paul here – what he needed, when he needed it, often at the very last minute! I used to think that God has a Plan A for my life – the 'right' job, house, spouse and so on. While I do believe he is interested in the minutiae of my life, I now believe that his main plan is a deep, lasting relationship with him. Everything else is secondary.

Corinth was a thriving port at the centre of world trade, known for its debauchery and for the huge temple of Aphrodite. Did Paul intend his usual plan – preach in the synagogue, make a few converts and then move on? He had to wait for the others (v 5) but then the usual pattern emerges, leading to opposition. Did he then want to depart? Travelling gets into the blood! But Paul has another vision, not to move on this time (Acts 16:9), but to stay put. I wonder how easy he found that.

One night the Lord spoke to Paul in a vision: 'Do not be afraid; keep on speaking, do not be silent.'

Acts 18:9

RESPOND

Pray: 'Lord, help me to be willing to ask for and wait for your guidance. And then to take it! Amen.'

Bible in a year: Proverbs 31; Psalm 94

Sunday 24 August
Psalm 52

A green olive tree

PREPARE
Pour a few drops of olive or other oil into a little container to help you reflect on this psalm.

READ
Psalm 52

EXPLORE
Think about your olive oil and where it grew. Maybe sniff it, swirl it around, notice its colour. Have you seen olive trees growing in Mediterranean countries? Their leaves are a distinctive grey-green evergreen, and turn silvery when the wind tosses them. It is a very strong, comparatively stocky tree, able to withstand the fiercest gales, and both the fruit and wood are useful. The pressed oil has historically had spiritual, culinary and medicinal uses – think of Moses sprinkling Aaron with oil, David being anointed by Samuel and the Good Samaritan using oil on wounds.

The olive is a significant tree in the Middle East. What was it to David (v 8)? Saul has tried to kill David several times, and now David has been betrayed after he ran away. Saul orders a massacre in retaliation (1 Samuel 21,22). David is intensely pained by all this evil (vs 1–4), but what gives him confidence (v 5)?

Olive trees grow fairly wide, due to their strong, massive root system. In contrast to the weak plant of the wicked enemy, which is easily uprooted, nothing can shake the solid olive tree. This was David's confidence because he was deeply rooted in the faithful and trustworthy God.

> But I am like an olive tree flourishing in the house of God; I trust in God's unfailing love for ever and ever.
>
> **Psalm 52:8**

RESPOND
Anoint your forehead, cross-shaped, with a little oil, as a precious reminder that you belong to God and are firmly rooted and grounded in him.

Bible in a year: Ecclesiastes 1–3; 2 Thessalonians 2

Monday 25 August

Acts 18:18–28

The ministry of others

PREPARE

Thank God for those who have shared the gospel and encouraged you in your Christian life. Be specific!

READ

Acts 18:18–28

EXPLORE

Apollos made a considerable impact, through God's grace, on the believers (v 27). Paul wrote, 'I planted the seed, Apollos watered it, but God has been making it grow' (1 Corinthians 3:6) when people said they preferred Apollos to Paul. And Luke attributes the impact of Apollos' ministry to God's grace alone.

Sometimes one notices in a church or group there's just one leader, keeping a firm control on everything and everyone. Or that someone is jealous of the ministry or work of another. What do you learn in these verses about how the early church worked?

They blessed the ministry of others, giving them the freedom to develop their part in God's work of grace. Far from limiting Apollos when he hadn't grasped the full implications of the gospel, it seems Aquila and Priscilla, themselves newly part of the ministry team, gently taught him and encouraged him (v 26).

How easy do you find it to do everything yourself and be in control? Take care: it can lead to burnout for you and it stifles the gifts and ministry of others who are also able through God's grace to be a part of the work. Paul has now added a number of people to his team and, far from finding that a threat, he can see that it has enabled the ministry to spread.

> When Apollos wanted to go to Achaia, the brothers and sisters encouraged him and wrote to the disciples there to welcome him. When he arrived, he was a great help to those who by grace had believed.
>
> **Acts 18:27**

RESPOND

Pray for your church leaders to have discernment in encouraging others.

Bible in a year: Ecclesiastes 4,5; 2 Thessalonians 3

Tuesday 26 August
Acts 19:1–22

It's magic!

PREPARE

Ask for the Holy Spirit to be powerfully at work in your life. What difference will it make to you and to others you know?

READ

Acts 19:1–22

EXPLORE

The people of Ephesus, an important city at the centre of ancient trade routes, liked power, and liked to make things happen. Ephesus was powerful in every way – including a powerful type of magic or sorcery (v 19). And so Luke, the author, emphasises the contrast of the power of the Holy Spirit, who is again at work in Paul's ministry. Where is the power of the Spirit most noticeable? Verses 6, 8 and 12. This is in stark contrast to the powers of magic and sorcery.

When the power of the Holy Spirit was seen, what were the effects (vs 17–20)? What a powerful impact indeed!

Where and when have you heard mention of 'sorcery' and belief in magic powers? Or even been impacted by them yourself? There are a variety of practices that need to be completely avoided by Christians, such as modern occultism, horoscopes, palm readings, Wicca, alternative spirituality, self-described wizards and witches, and so on. Such beliefs are all flourishing and many, particularly young, people are drawn into such practices, especially when exploring spirituality and other 'powers' online. How might you pray for people you know, to be protected from such power and to resist its fascination?

> In this way the word of the Lord spread widely and grew in power.
>
> **Acts 19:20**

RESPOND

Pray for the Spirit's powerful protection in the lives of people in your family and at your church who may be drawn away from God towards spiritual practices or beliefs which have a negative impact on them.

Bible in a year: Ecclesiastes 6,7; Psalms 95,96

Wednesday 27 August

Acts 19:23–41

Challenging the world

PREPARE

Pray: 'Lord Jesus, help me to turn the world upside down for you, through the power of your Holy Spirit. Amen.'

READ

Acts 19:23–41

EXPLORE

Walking the streets of Ephesus today, one imagines the enormous, bustling city it once was, with vast statues of gods and goddesses and the Roman Emperor; fountains and public toilets; a majestic library; thriving shops and businesses. A meteorite had once landed nearby, thought to be the goddess Artemis (Diana to the Romans). Many made their living from her and were exceedingly disgruntled when Paul said that man-made gods are no gods at all. Their livelihood was threatened, and maybe underneath it all they wondered if their man-made gods were not real – they feared being exposed. They were certainly able to stir up enough anxiety to incite the hysterical crowd to chant and riot for several hours. What an impact Paul's words made! Do your words, actions or life have any impact on those around you?

Perhaps, for many of us, it's been all too easy to be sucked into the world's way of viewing things, to stay quiet when others use God's name for swearing, or to ignore behaviours that go against God's ways. Can we speak out against the world's views, even if it means losing our friends? What do you need from the Holy Spirit to stand strong?

'... Paul has convinced and led astray large numbers of people here ... He says that gods made by human hands are no gods at all.'

Acts 19:26

RESPOND

Prayerfully reflect on Romans 12:2: 'Do not conform to the pattern of this world, but be transformed by the renewing of your mind. Then you will be able to test and approve what God's will is – his good, pleasing and perfect will.'

Bible in a year: Ecclesiastes 8,9; 1 Timothy 1

Thursday 28 August

Acts 20:1–12

How long?

PREPARE

Be aware of the Lord's presence with you. Open yourself to what he wants to say. Take all the time you need.

READ

Acts 20:1–12

EXPLORE

Do you like epic films, such as *Lord of the Rings* or *Avatar*? Lengthy, all-absorbing adventures? We're a very sedentary generation, and we'll sit for long films but not always for times with the Lord or for lengthy sermons! Someone once said that what orators lack in depth they make up for in length. I can't think that was true of Paul, who, knowing he was on the move, wanted to ensure he shared as much as possible with his audience. Even Eutychus' accident didn't stop him speaking right through the night. And no one is mentioned as leaving.

I'm reminded of how little time I actually spend going deeper in my love for and knowledge of the Lord. How I race through my daily readings or cut short my prayers, or hope the preacher isn't too long on Sunday because I've things to do and places to go and people to meet. Does that resonate with you too?

What might need to change in your attitude to both length and depth in your time with the Lord?

> The people took the young man home alive and were greatly comforted.
>
> **Acts 20:12**

RESPOND

Think about your priorities. When could you have a longer time, what would that involve? A walk; reading an epistle in one sitting; listening to a podcast or sermon; maybe going on retreat? What needs to be put in the diary/schedule so it happens?

Bible in a year: Ecclesiastes 10,11; 1 Timothy 2

Friday 29 August
Acts 20:13–24

Just one thing

PREPARE
Pray: 'Lord, I know sometimes/often you aren't the most important thing in my life. Please forgive me and fill me with your Spirit. Amen.'

READ
Acts 20:13–24

EXPLORE
Did you ever watch *City Slickers*, a film about some city men who go on vacation out west to learn to be cowboys? The rancher holds up one finger to tell them the secret to life: it's just one thing.

'I'm not indispensable; I just want to go on doing what God has called me to – telling everyone I meet about the extravagant grace of God' (my translation of verse 24). Here is Paul's one thing. In spite of all the difficulties and pain he's experienced, in spite of knowing there's more to come, Paul is determined to follow God's calling on his life and carry on spreading the good news. The power of the Holy Spirit is still filling him as Ananias had said it would (Acts 9:17).

What's your 'one thing'? Money or job; family or friends; possessions or desires? Or something else entirely? If you're absolutely honest, what matters most? What fills your time, your attention, your mind? And how important are you – does your life matter to you?

'However, I consider my life worth nothing to me; my only aim is to finish the race and complete the task the Lord Jesus has given me – the task of testifying to the good news of God's grace.'

Acts 20:24

RESPOND
Allow the Spirit to show you what's most important to you, being open and honest with yourself. Are confession and repentance needed? A refilling with the Holy Spirit? A rededication to the things of the Lord? A finding of your true one thing?

Bible in a year: Ecclesiastes 12; 1 Timothy 3

Saturday 30 August
Acts 20:25–38

The power of a blessing

PREPARE

What does 'blessing someone' mean to you?

READ

Acts 20:25–38

EXPLORE

A young mother came into Bath Abbey, pushing her baby in a stroller. I smiled and asked how old the little one was. 'Just three weeks,' the mother replied. 'May I pray a blessing over her?' I asked. The mother's attitude changed immediately, declining my offer rather coldly, hastily moving on. I was mystified; it's not very often that anyone refuses prayer, let alone a blessing.

Shortly afterwards, I led the hourly prayers and ended, 'A final blessing for you and those you love.' And I raised my hand as I prayed a blessing over the people in the abbey. Afterwards, the young mother came to find me. 'Is that what you meant by a prayer of blessing?' she asked. 'Because I'd like that for the baby.' It made me realise that our 'Christian jargon' is not understood by many non-churchgoers. Yet as I prayed a blessing, the mother's face softened, she thanked me and took the 'Why Jesus?' booklet that I offered her.

Praying blessings on others is a rich privilege, and one that we often forget about. Paul prayed strong blessings on people – here in verse 32 and in his letters to churches. We too can pray blessings on everyone.

> 'Now I commit you to God and to the word of his grace, which can build you up and give you an inheritance among all those who are sanctified.'
> **Acts 20:32**

RESPOND

Use Paul's words in verse 32 to bless someone, or Ephesians 1:17–19 or 2 Thessalonians 2:16,17, for example. You might pray it now, or later you could send it in an email or letter, or even pray it with them in person.

Bible in a year: Song of Songs 1,2; Psalms 97,98

Sunday 31 August

Psalm 53

Whose fool are you?

PREPARE

'This is the day the Lord has made; let us rejoice and be glad in it' (Psalm 118:24, ESV). How might you do that now?

READ

Psalm 53

EXPLORE

Our psalm today classes fools as those who say there is no God (v 1). Proverbs 28:26 talks about how a fool trusts in his own understanding. When foolishness pervades one's life, the consequences can be very serious. The Psalmist talks about God putting them to shame (v 5). Was there ever a time when you said 'there is no God'? If there was, what was it that persuaded you otherwise? What might you learn from that, as you think about being witnesses and mission in our context?

Most of us do not enjoy being called or taken for a fool, and playing an April Fool's joke on someone can be met with a very mixed reception.

We cannot always avoid any of these things happening to us; there are sometimes people who will call us a fool for our beliefs, or our kindness, or the way we seem to live out our Christian faith.

But we are wise (v 2), not foolish, in God's eyes, if we seek after him. What does seeking God look like for you at the moment? There may be times when we end up looking foolish to others as we do that but, ultimately, it is God's view that matters.

God looks down from heaven on all mankind to see if there are any who understand, any who seek God.

Psalm 53:2

RESPOND

Do you know anyone who categorically believes there is no God? Rather than calling them a fool, how can you be praying for them? Don't forget yesterday's idea of blessing others as well.

Bible in a year: Song of Songs 3,4; 1 Timothy 4

Love is the greatest

About the writer
Suzy Pearson

Suzy is a vicar in the West Midlands, where she lives with her husband and two young children. She enjoys running, cycling, reading and spending time with her family.

The prophet Hosea lived during a tumultuous time in the history of Israel. They had become a divided kingdom and, with Jeroboam II (one of the worst kings of Israel) on the throne, they were headed for destruction. God had delivered them from slavery in Egypt, provided for them and led them to the Promised Land, but they had strayed from the covenant that God had made with them at Sinai and had worshipped other gods.

The book of Hosea uses marriage as a metaphor to explore the relationship of covenant between God and Israel. A common interpretation of this metaphor positions Gomer, Hosea's wife, as representing unfaithful Israel and Hosea as symbolising God. Like all metaphors, this metaphor has limitations and care must be taken not to make problematic extrapolations. Unfortunately, this text has been used to oppress people, particularly women. There may be parts of the readings this week that you find uncomfortable. Before we begin this week's reflections, I want to make clear that the metaphor is not about shaming people who have had extra-marital affairs. It is not about dismissing the pain caused by unfaithfulness. It is not about endorsing slavery or human trafficking. It is not about blaming women as the root of corruption. It is not about God orchestrating suffering for the purposes of a sermon illustration. Rather, it is about the relentless love of God towards each one of us and our response.

Monday 1 September

Hosea 1:1 – 2:1

God in Gomer

PREPARE

Take a moment to recall people or situations that have shown you something about the character of God. What did they teach you? As you enter prayer now, thank God for these characteristics and for revealing them to you.

READ

Hosea 1:1 – 2:1

EXPLORE

The Bible is full of examples of God working through people and situations that we find surprising. We often see God in places that we might not expect, seem unlikely or cause us (or the religious leaders of the day) to raise our eyebrows. Perhaps you were surprised to read that God told Hosea to 'marry a promiscuous woman'. It doesn't sound like the advice you might expect to hear in church.

The woman who is chosen is Gomer. She gives birth to three children and one is named Lo-Ruhamah, meaning 'not loved'. But notice in verse 8 it says, 'After she had weaned Lo-Ruhamah…'. This little verse shows us that Gomer nursed her child, nurtured her and protected her. She loved her daughter, regardless of what was said about her. It is through Gomer that God's purposes are brought about and we see God's love demonstrated.

It wouldn't be the last time that God chooses a woman in unlikely circumstances to do this. Many years later, a young woman in Nazareth would be chosen by God to carry a child to reveal God's love.

… 'Go, marry a promiscuous woman and have children with her, for like an adulterous wife this land is guilty of unfaithfulness to the LORD.'

Hosea 1:2

RESPOND

Where do you see God at work through surprising people or situations? Pray that God would remove any prejudice and help you to be aware of and open to God at work today.

Bible in a year: Song of Songs 5,6; 1 Timothy 5

Tuesday 2 September

Hosea 2:2–23

Faith in the Creator

PREPARE

'Through him all things were made; without him nothing was made that has been made' (John 1:3). Give thanks for all that God has created and provided for you.

READ

Hosea 2:2–23

EXPLORE

In today's reading, Hosea highlights how Israel has been unfaithful to God by offering worship to Baal. Baal (meaning 'master' or 'husband') was the Canaanite god of fertility and rainstorms. As an agrarian society in an arid climate, Israel was dependent on both of these at the best of times.

But this was the worst of times. There was political unrest, economic hardship and trade instability. No doubt anything that would bolster their reserves would have appealed – anything to increase their crop yield, expand their flocks and grow their population to strengthen their defence; literally anything – even if it meant not living according to the values that God had called them to live by, even if it meant exploiting the poorest and employing unfair work practices. So, instead of seeking God earnestly, they look to the Canaanite Baals to provide for them. They 'forget' that it is God who is the Creator of the rain and causes all things to grow.

'I will plant her for myself in the land; I will show my love to the one I called "Not my loved one". I will say to those called "Not my people", "You are my people"; and they will say, "You are my God."'

Hosea 2:23

RESPOND

When times are tough, it can be challenging to depend on God and not place hope elsewhere. What do you turn to when times are tough? Does it compromise your faithfulness to God? Ask God to help you live faithfully today.

Bible in a year: Song of Songs 7,8; Psalms 99–101

Wednesday 3 September
Hosea 3:1–5

Non-controlling love

PREPARE

Slow your breathing and focus on your breath. As you inhale, breathe in love. As you exhale, breathe out love for others. Repeat, using words such as peace, hope, joy, faith or the fruits of the Spirit.

READ

Hosea 3:1–5

EXPLORE

Whenever anyone uses an analogy in which they may be seen as representing God, I am a little suspicious of how they understand their power in relation to others. So when I read the book of Hosea, it does alarm me that Hosea might have seen himself as taking on the role of God in his relationship with Gomer. But perhaps by doing so it reveals that God loves in a very different way to how Hosea thinks God loves.

Notice that the instruction God gives in verse 1 is to Hosea and is about how Hosea should love. It is not about how Gomer should love and neither does God tell Hosea that he should force Gomer to behave in a certain way. Nevertheless, Hosea takes it upon himself to tell Gomer how he thinks she should behave. Hosea might think he is loving Gomer the way that God loves, but actually he is not. Coercive control is not love – it is abuse. In contrast, the love of God is non-controlling, non-coercive. God's love for us does not falter or depend on our actions – it is unconditional.

> Then I told her, 'You are to live with me for many days; you must not be a prostitute or be intimate with any man, and I will behave the same way toward you.'
>
> **Hosea 3:3**

RESPOND

If possible, look up the lyrics for the hymn 'Let Love Be Real' by Michael Forster (or even better, listen to it too) and use these words or 1 Corinthians 13 as a prayer.

Bible in a year: Isaiah 1,2; 1 Timothy 6

Thursday 4 September
Hosea 6:1 - 7:2

Love languages

PREPARE
Offer to God those things that concern you today. You might find it helpful to hold clenched fists in front of you and then release them open to God as you pray.

READ
Hosea 6:1 - 7:2

EXPLORE
When my now husband and I were preparing to get married, we were asked if we knew what our 'love languages' were and if we knew each other's. It sparked a 'debate' between us about how I had thoughtfully, or so I had thought, bought us theatre tickets as a surprise for his birthday. It turned out that John did not like surprises and what he appreciated most about birthdays was being able to specify what he wanted. I could pretend that this was the last time that we've had crossed wires but 16 years on, it's happened quite a few more times!

Fortunately, it's not this complicated where God is concerned. God sees our heart. God sees our intentions. We do not need to package our love for God in particular ways. Equally, nothing gets past God. God sees our inner motives hidden beneath our outer performance – when we're doing the sacrifices and the burnt offerings, as it were, but it doesn't match up with our desires (v 6). God knows when our 'love is like the morning mist, like the early dew that disappears' (v 4).

> 'For I desire mercy, not sacrifice, and acknowledgment of God rather than burnt offerings.'
>
> **Hosea 6:6**

RESPOND
What does God see in your heart? What motivates you? Is there anything that you try to keep hidden? Pray: 'Holy God, make my love for you steadfast. Amen.'

Bible in a year: Isaiah 3–5; 2 Timothy 1

Friday 5 September
Hosea 11:1–11

Divine parent love

PREPARE

Read this summary of Romans 8, verses 38 and 39 several times slowly: 'Nothing can ever come between us and the love of God.' Try placing the emphasis on a different word each time you read it.

READ

Hosea 11:1–11

EXPLORE

In today's passage, God is depicted as a parent who has taught, nurtured and fed Israel. How we relate to this may depend on our own experiences of being parented, being parents or the absence of these relationships in our lives. I have two young children and sometimes they do things that I have asked them not to do. Usually, after a while, they say sorry and we chat about what they can do to remedy the situation and what they would do differently next time. While I would like for them to learn from the situation, what I really want is for them to know that I love them. If that is my desire as a very imperfect parent, how much more does God as the perfect parent desire this for us?

In verse 9, God says, 'I will not carry out my fierce anger … For I am God'. God's very nature is love. God sees everything – the things we have said, done and thought – and loves us. Nothing is or can be hidden from God.

> 'I led them with cords of human kindness, with ties of love. To them I was like one who lifts a little child to the cheek, and I bent down to feed them.'
>
> **Hosea 11:4**

RESPOND

Are there things that you have said, done or thought that you like to keep hidden? How does it feel to know that God sees it all and still loves you? Pray: 'Loving God, help me to experience your love for me today. Amen.'

Bible in a year: Isaiah 6,7; 2 Timothy 2

Saturday 6 September

Hosea 14:1–9

The end is not the end

PREPARE

Look back at the readings for this week and thank God for any insights that have been revealed to you.

READ

Hosea 14:1–9

EXPLORE

The book of Hosea ends with a poem that beckons Israel to repent and describes what the healed Israel will be like – a tree providing shade for people to dwell beneath its branches. There is then a short note (v 9), probably written by the editor after Hosea's prophecies had been collated. The editor's message is not directed at Israel but at us, the reader.

We, reading these prophecies now, know that Israel did in fact fall to the Assyrian Empire after Hosea's prophecies. Was this because they did not repent? Did they repent? We don't know – the editor doesn't say. Neither are we told what comes of Hosea and Gomer's marriage. Perhaps it is no coincidence that Gomer's name means 'sudden end'.

As we often experience in life, we are left with an unresolved situation and have to live with the tension of not knowing why something happened. It seems that the editor is intentional about leaving us with this incomplete ending. Instead, he invites us to continue the narrative – to discern the truth about God's character from the text and respond to God's invitation. There is a lot in life that we don't know, but what we can know is that God is with us in the uncertainty.

'Who is wise? Let them realise these things. Who is discerning? Let them understand. The ways of the LORD are right; the righteous walk in them, but the rebellious stumble in them.'

Hosea 14:9

RESPOND

Are there situations in your life that feel unresolved? Pray that you would be aware of God with you in the present circumstances.

Bible in a year: Isaiah 8,9; Psalm 102

Sunday 7 September
Psalm 54

God of justice

PREPARE

Recall times in your life where you have experienced God as your helper. Give thanks to God for being with you and sustaining you.

READ

Psalm 54

EXPLORE

When I read aloud a psalm such as this, I often squirm a little as I ask God to destroy my enemies. It feels uncomfortable to be heard asking for something that appears to be at odds with Jesus' teaching to love one's enemies. However, I started to see it differently when I read it through the eyes of a victim of injustice.

I wonder if you have ever been a victim of injustice. It can be a very painful and disorientating experience, in which one can feel powerless or unsure as to how to use what power one has. The words of Psalm 54 can be a helpful prayer in such situations. The structure of this seven-versed psalm intentionally places verse 4 at the centre: 'Surely God is my help; the Lord is the one who sustains me.' The verses surrounding it demonstrate that we can express to God our pain, our frustrations, our anger and our desires for an end to injustice.

We can trust in God our helper and sustainer to enact justice perfectly.

Surely God is my help; the Lord is the one who sustains me.

Psalm 54:4

RESPOND

Where do you see injustice happening today? It might be events happening in other countries or it might be situations that you personally are involved with. Use Psalm 54 as a template to pray to God about them.

Bible in a year: Isaiah 10–12; 2 Timothy 3

Mark 8:27 – 10:52

The journey of discipleship

Discipleship is an exciting call. Following Jesus, the way Jesus wants us to follow him, is at the same time both a blessed experience and a risky task.

Dietrich Bonhoeffer, in his 1937 classic book *The Cost of Discipleship*, reminds us of the joys and adventures of Christian life. For those who willingly submit to the purpose and plan of God, the yoke they are called to bear can be easy and the burden light (Matthew 11:30).

About the writer
Vinod Victor

Vinod is the chaplain of the Anglican Church in Freiburg and the Area Dean of Germany. He is also chair of CMS-Asia. Before moving to Germany, Vinod served in various congregations in India and Australia, and has a history of ecumenical and missional engagement.

Even as Jesus prepares his disciples for the exciting journey with him, he makes it very clear that those who follow him will always be in the shadow of the cross. They may be blamed, hated, condemned and called fanatics. There could be temptations to desert the Lord and even risks to life. Yet Jesus, who never forsakes his dear ones, carries their burdens and gives strength and courage to bear the cross. Ultimately it is, however, a story of hope and triumph.

Mark chapters 9 and 10 are about Jesus equipping the disciples to understand the essence of following him. It touches upon key themes like faith, marriage, riches and servanthood and has some wonderful stories of healing. The forewarnings of Jesus about his passion and death are juxtaposed with the disciples' quest for power and authority. The invitation to take a closer look at Jesus, as the life-pattern to emulate, runs through these chapters. We will hear stories that help us on our own journey of discipleship.

Monday 8 September

Mark 8:27–30

Who do you say I am?

PREPARE

Imagine Jesus meets you on your way and asks you a simple question: 'How about you? Who do you say I am?' What would be your response?

READ

Mark 8:27–30

EXPLORE

Two young children were having a conversation. One had an orange in his hand, and he asked his friend, 'How does this orange taste?' The friend responded, 'How would I know unless I taste it myself?'

This experience is true in our God encounters too. Unless we taste and see who Jesus is in our lives, it will not be easy to answer the question of who is this Jesus we talk about every day. While it may be easy to say who others say Jesus is, when it becomes a personal question it requires a deep inner search to respond meaningfully.

For others, Jesus could be a prophet, a good human being, the Saviour of humankind, the Alpha and Omega, the Living Stone – but the crucial question is: What about you; who do *you* say he is?

Peter, when asked this question, had no doubt in his mind when he declared, 'You are the Messiah' (v 29). It was his experience, his firm conviction and the realisation he encountered, thanks to the revelation of the Holy Spirit, through his close walk with Jesus.

'Who do you say I am?'

Mark 8:29

RESPOND

Pray: 'Help me, O Lord, to boldly declare to the world who you are in my life.' Who can you share this with this week?

Bible in a year: Isaiah 13,14; 2 Timothy 4

Tuesday 9 September

Mark 8:31 – 9:1

How precious is our soul?

PREPARE

Reflect on your decision or realisation that you wanted to follow Jesus. What difference did it make to your life?

READ

Mark 8:31 – 9:1

EXPLORE

Today's passage begins with Jesus challenging his disciples with the insight that, if they want to be his followers, they need to deny themselves, take up their cross and follow him (v 34). Is this a message you heard when you decided to follow Jesus? What do you think gets in the way of people following Jesus today?

Jesus then goes on to ask the disciples what good it is for someone to gain the whole world yet forfeit their soul (v 36). Other translations, such as the NRSV, use the word 'life' instead of 'soul', which perhaps makes it clearer that gaining the whole world and losing your life is a foolish endeavour.

Further, Jesus goes on to ask what they can give in return for their life which hints at what his death and resurrection will accomplish – as Christians we have eternal life because of what Jesus has done.

The passage finishes with a warning about being ashamed of Jesus and his words – something that is important to consider as we seek to live out our Christian lives. How do people know that you are a Christian?

'Or what can anyone give in exchange for their soul?'

Mark 8:37

RESPOND

What does it mean for you, today, to deny yourself, take up your cross and follow Jesus? Is there one action you think God is calling you to today?

Bible in a year: Isaiah 15,16; Psalm 103

Wednesday 10 September
Mark 9:2–13

A mountaintop experience

PREPARE

Reflect on some of your mountaintop experiences with Jesus. Which memory stands out most strongly?

READ

Mark 9:2–13

EXPLORE

I wonder what Peter, James and John were expecting when Jesus led them up a mountain (v 2). I would be surprised if they expected what followed – Jesus transfigured and in conversation with Moses and Elijah (v 4). I wonder how they recognised them. Perhaps they recalled the stories of Moses encountering God on Mount Sinai (Exodus 32–34). Has your journey with Jesus led you to any surprising or unexpected places or encounters? Peter didn't know what to say. He was terrified (v 6, ESV) and suggested building a dwelling for each of them, perhaps echoing the tabernacle in the wilderness where God dwelt. I wonder what you would have done in Peter's place. Then a voice from above announced that Jesus was the beloved Son (v 7, ESV), an echo of God's words at his baptism (Mark 1:11, ESV).

As they descended the mountain, Jesus prohibited them from talking about their experience and again talked about his death and resurrection (v 9), which the disciples still did not understand (v 10). How hard might it have been not to share such an experience? How do we know whether or not to share with people some of our intimate moments with God? Jesus then confirms the belief that Elijah will return (Malachi 3:1) but also alludes to John the Baptist as a prophet like Elijah (v 13). A thought-provoking experience.

After six days Jesus took Peter, James and John with him and led them up a high mountain, where they were all alone.

Mark 9:2

RESPOND

Pray: 'Lord Jesus, open our eyes to see you, our ears to hear you and our hearts to behold you.'

Bible in a year: Isaiah 17–20; Titus 1

Thursday 11 September

Mark 9:14–29

If you can?

PREPARE

Have you ever encountered a situation where you thought it was beyond even God to be able to help? Yet with fumbling words have you dared to say, 'Lord, if you can...'?

READ

Mark 9:14–29

EXPLORE

A story is told of Jenny, living in a remote village, who was worried that her eyesight was deteriorating each day. Everything was turning blurred for her. When it was time for shoebox gifts at Christmas, the village children were excited. Jenny was praying, 'Lord, if you can, please restore my sight. I want to see again.' When the gifts were handed out, surprisingly there was a pair of spectacles in Jenny's box and she was astonished that, when she wore them, she could see perfectly. Jenny was amazed at God's provision.

In today's passage, God's provision for the father of the boy with seizures comes through the power and authority of Jesus, who is able to free the child from the evil spirit (v 25). There will be a range of different perspectives on this story today, and exorcism can be a controversial and potentially abusive practice. The important thing for us to focus on is that Jesus responded with compassion to a father who was distressed over his child and was perhaps seeing Jesus as his last resort. The story is another piece in the jigsaw of Jesus demonstrating that he is the Son of God.

Immediately the boy's father exclaimed, 'I do believe; help me overcome my unbelief!'

Mark 9:24

RESPOND

What are you struggling to believe at the moment? Ask God to help you overcome your unbelief.

Bible in a year: Isaiah 21,22; Titus 2

Friday 12 September
Mark 9:30–37

Greatness of the last

PREPARE

Think back to conversations you have had about who is or was the greatest or the best. What was at the root of them?

READ

Mark 9:30–37

EXPLORE

The king and the queen of the little kingdom were overwhelmed when the prince came back from a visit to a remote village and told his parents that he had found his future queen. The entourage immediately set out to see the would-be bride, but were surprised to find the very humble home of a peasant and a charming young lady. The prince said, 'I watched the women fetching water at the village well. This girl came first but allowed all the other women to fetch water before her and even helped several of them to do so. After everyone had filled their pitchers, she filled hers and walked home.'

Jesus tells his disciples yet again of his impending dying and rising again, and verse 32 says that the disciples were afraid to ask what he meant. Are there things that you are afraid of asking God about or things that you are struggling to understand?

But on the way back the argument the disciples had was not about what Jesus said but about who was the greatest among them.

Is there anything distracting you from serving God at this time? As Jesus taught, greatness is never in being the first or the best, but instead it is in the willingness to be the last and in the joy one finds in serving others.

'Anyone who wants to be first must be the very last, and the servant of all.'

Mark 9:35

RESPOND

Pray: 'Teach me, O Lord, to understand the mystery of finding joy in serving and satisfaction in allowing others to be first.'

Bible in a year: Isaiah 23,24; Titus 3

Saturday 13 September
Mark 9:38–50

Losing our saltiness

PREPARE

Have you ever come across salt that has lost its saltiness? Have you imagined that it could be your story too? What might it mean in your life?

READ

Mark 9:38–50

EXPLORE

When the disciples tried to stop someone from doing miracles in the name of Jesus, he told them that those who are not against us are for us (v 40) and warned everyone not to be stumbling blocks in the way of others (v 42). What have been some of the stumbling blocks you have experienced or you see being put in the way of people following Jesus today?

When the Gospel of Mark was written, salt was a valuable commodity, much more than something that gave food its flavour. It was used as a preservative; important when there were no refrigerators. It acted as a disinfectant too, as it still does today. It was offered as part of some sacrifices and it symbolised a covenant. Imagine if salt lost its properties to do all of these things. That could be very challenging! It helps us see why Jesus used this analogy to warn his disciples not to lose their saltiness – a distinct possibility.

Jesus urges them to always have salt among themselves. The sign of having salt within us is living at peace with each other (v 50).

'Salt is good, but if it loses its saltiness, how can you make it salty again? Have salt among yourselves, and be at peace with each other.'

Mark 9:50

RESPOND

Pray: 'Help me, O Lord, never to lose my saltiness and always to live in peace with others.'

Bible in a year: Isaiah 25,26; Psalm 104

Sunday 14 September

Psalm 55

When friends betray

PREPARE

How do we respond when we realise that close friends are not on the same side as us over an issue?

READ

Psalm 55

EXPLORE

William Shakespeare portrays the assassination of Julius Caesar in a very dramatic manner in his play with the same title. As the conspirators gather around Caesar at the Senate on the Ides of March, he is literally taken aback to see his close friend and associate Brutus to be among them. Caesar's last words, according to Shakespeare, were 'Et tu, Brute?', which literally means 'You too, Brutus?'. An alternative is put forward by Cassius Dio, who suggests the words may have been 'You too, son?' When family or close friends betray us, it is indeed heartbreaking.

The pain of the psalmist is seen in verses 12 to 15, as he laments over his close friend. In 2 Samuel 15:31, David is being told, 'Ahithophel is among the conspirators with Absalom.' This could be the context in which David writes this psalm. The anguish of the heart is not only about the fear of death and the horror that was overwhelming, but also from the fact that his opponents are those David would have never imagined to be betrayers. He, however, trusts the Lord will give him strength to face such difficult situations (v 22), and this trust in God's saving and sustaining power is threaded through the last eight verses.

> Cast your cares on the Lord and he will sustain you; he will never let the righteous be shaken.
>
> **Psalm 55:22**

RESPOND

Pray: 'Lord, help me to never be a betrayer. When I experience betrayal, help me to trust in you for the strength I need to sustain me.'

Bible in a year: Isaiah 27,28; Philemon 1

Monday 15 September

Mark 10:1–12

Can one plus one still be one?

PREPARE

When two individuals are united in holy matrimony, have you ever considered what it costs for the two to become one?

READ

Mark 10:1–12

EXPLORE

While solemnising a marriage, the minister read from the Bible and told the young couple, 'You are no longer two but one. Do you think that it is possible?' Blinded by love though they were, their eyes did have a look of wonder. The minister said, 'Imagine two wonderful rivers flowing from two directions. At one point the two rivers merge and then flow together. One plus one has now become a bigger one and that is the mystery of marriage. Each of these rivers carries with it all its richness and merges into the richness of the other and together they form an entirely new and beautiful entity.'

Jesus herein gives some wonderful insights about marriage, in response to a question from the Pharisees about divorce (vs 7–9). Why do you think the Pharisees asked this question? Marriage calls for prayerful giving up, thoughtful adjustments and intentional initiatives; not the hardness of heart that led to Moses permitting divorce (v 5). The affirmation that it is God who joins people together not only adds to the spiritual dimension of marriage but also points at the responsibility of the partners in safeguarding and protecting marriages as sacred. The passage is another example of the disciples seeking clarity in private on something Jesus taught in public (vs 10–12). Does it raise questions for you?

'Therefore what God has joined together, let no one separate.'

Mark 10:9

RESPOND

Pray for those who are struggling in their marriages at the moment, as well as those who are feeling the loss of bereavement or divorce, or are experiencing unwanted singleness.

Bible in a year: Isaiah 29,30; Hebrews 1

Tuesday 16 September
Mark 10:13–16

Being like children

PREPARE

Think about what good qualities of being a child we lose with ageing.

READ

Mark 10:13–16

EXPLORE

Children can be much wiser than we think and we sometimes underestimate their spiritual wisdom. A chaplain tells of how they were using nesting dolls with a child and she asked the question 'Which one is God? Is it the smallest one who lives inside of me or the biggest one who holds all the others?' What wisdom from a child has surprised you?

When Jesus tells his disciples that anyone who will not receive the kingdom of God like a little child will never enter it, he is, in fact, urging all of them to keep thinking of the child-like qualities that people sometimes lose as they age. These could be qualities that are crucial for the kingdom culture that Jesus is envisaging. The invitation of Jesus has not only been 'Let the children come' but is also 'Come to me as children would.'

The words and actions of Jesus here may have been particularly shocking to those listening, because of the low status of children. Children were powerless, and it would not have been obvious how the kingdom could come through powerlessness, not more traditional forceful means. But in powerlessness there is only God to depend on.

And he took the children in his arms, placed his hands on them and blessed them.

Mark 10:16

RESPOND

Pray: 'Help me, Lord, not to stand in the way of our children experiencing the beauty of having Jesus as their friend. Help me, Lord, to come to you as a child would.'

Bible in a year: Isaiah 31,32; Psalm 105

Wednesday 17 September

Mark 10:17–31

Riches in heaven

PREPARE

Where is our investment? Is it here on earth or is it up above?

READ

Mark 10:17–31

EXPLORE

The legend of King Gondoforos, well known in my eastern culture, speaks of how he invited an apostle who was a carpenter to build a castle for him. Instead of building the castle, the apostle distributed the money provided to the poor. When the king summoned him, the apostle answered that the castle for the king is already ready in heaven. The furious king imprisoned the apostle. The same night, the king dreamed that he was at the pearly gates. He was shown a beautiful house and was told, 'This is what you have invested while you lived on earth.' The king woke up from his dream and ordered the immediate release of the apostle and dedicated the rest of his life to the service of the poor and the ordinary.

In asking what he had to do to inherit eternal life (v 17), I wonder what the rich man was expecting Jesus to say. Perhaps he was hoping that his keeping of the commandments would be enough (v 20). We do not hear whether or not the rich man did do as Jesus told him to do. It is one of the many unanswered questions in the Bible! What do you think?

Jesus says, 'all things are possible with God' (v 27). We may not always know the impact of words spoken and how they may later bear fruit.

'It is easier for a camel to go through the eye of a needle than for someone who is rich to enter the kingdom of God.'

Mark 10:25

RESPOND

Pray: 'Help me, O Lord, to see the riches of the kingdom of God more than the riches of this world.'

Bible in a year: Isaiah 33,34; Hebrews 2

Thursday 18 September
Mark 10:32–34

The shadow of the cross

PREPARE

What are the risks of discipleship for you today? What is helping or hindering you moving forward?

READ

Mark 10:32–34

EXPLORE

The story of Christianity is also a story of many martyrs, such as Eric Liddell (the film *Chariots of Fire* tells his story). The Olympic athlete and missionary knew he faced an uncertain future in China but still chose to go, in the same way that Jesus, here, chooses to continue to Jerusalem (v 32). Have there been points in your journey where it has been hard to choose to continue?

In every missionary journey there is the constant presence of the shadow of the cross – the knowledge of being called to follow Jesus and that the following is costly and may embrace suffering or even death, as Jesus explains to his disciples in this passage. As Jesus walks up to Jerusalem with his disciples, he is aware of what is awaiting him (vs 33,34). He makes it known to the twelve that tough days are inevitable, but also gives them the larger picture of the salvation narrative. Those who follow are afraid because it is a known fact that a conspiracy is being hatched to get rid of Jesus.

Here, Jesus is giving them a realistic picture of discipleship. It is going to be costly. Was that clear to you when you began to follow Jesus? There are many places around the world where choosing to follow Jesus is a risky option and the shadow of the cross is apparent.

'Three days later he will rise.'

Mark 10:34

RESPOND

Pray: 'Help me, Lord, to constantly see the shadow of the cross in my journey of discipleship.'

Bible in a year: Isaiah 35,36; Hebrews 3

Friday 19 September

Mark 10:35–45

Not to be served but to serve

PREPARE

Think about your expectations as you follow Christ. In what ways are they biblically shaped?

READ

Mark 10:35–45

EXPLORE

Bishop Jesudasan was once approached by church leaders. They were debating what image of Christ should be featured on the central stained glass window, which was costing a lot of money. After listening to them, the bishop asked, 'Why do you want to spend so much when the needs of the last, the least and the lost around you are so great?' Noticing the silence in the room, he continued: 'Jesus came to serve and if you want to look at an image that would challenge the people then look at a servant image of Jesus. Why not a simple image of Jesus washing the feet of his disciples with a towel around his waist?'

James and John were surely thinking about a Messianic kingdom 'here and now' when they came to Jesus saying, 'We want you to do for us whatever we ask' (v 35). What they wanted were the prime positions on the left and the right of Jesus. 'These places belong to those for whom they have been prepared', Jesus told them (v 40), and reminded them again that 'whoever wants to become great among you must be your servant, and whoever wants to be first must be slave of all' (vs 43,44).

'For even the Son of Man did not come to be served, but to serve, and to give his life as a ransom for many.'

Mark 10:45

RESPOND

Pray that God will help you to follow the model of Jesus who was ever willing to serve and never wanted to be served.

Bible in a year: Isaiah 37,38; Hebrews 4

Saturday 20 September
Mark 10:46–52

Jesus' question

PREPARE

What helps us really see? How do we look with more than just our eyes?

READ

Mark 10:46–52

EXPLORE

'Let every veil that blinds us from seeing the design of God for our lives be lifted so that we can dance the divine choreography,' the pastor said as he was teaching about prayer. One person quipped, 'But I am not blind; I can see.' The pastor smiled and asked him, 'Are you sure? Can you really see? Do not forget that sometimes people with vision challenges can see with their hearts more clearly than those who think they can see. A wise thing to do is to constantly pray: Lord, I want to see.'

Bartimaeus heard that Jesus was coming to town and so he shouted out to him for mercy. Though the crowd tried to hush him he caught the attention of Jesus who called him near. Throwing aside his cloak, Bartimaeus came to Jesus and Jesus asked him, 'What do you want me to do for you?' That is a very challenging question for Jesus to ask – it does not always have an obvious answer, although it did in this case. If Jesus asked you that question today, what would your response be? Would you look to respond 'Lord, I want to see' with Bartimaeus, or would it be something else? As we ponder this question, do we think there is a difference between what we want and what God sees that we need?

'What do you want me to do for you?' Jesus asked him. The blind man said, 'Rabbi, I want to see.'

Mark 10:51

RESPOND

Pray: 'Help me, O Lord, to have the right answer when Jesus asks me next time: "What do you want me to do for you?"'

Bible in a year: Isaiah 39,40; Psalm 106

Sunday 21 September

Psalm 56

God who knows our tears

PREPARE

When the going gets tough, how does God show his love and care for you?

READ

Psalm 56

EXPLORE

The psalmist was having a tough patch in his life. The Philistines had successfully pursued and perhaps reached him (v 1). Despite this, there is a positive note of hope that fills this psalm, best seen in the final section where the psalmist affirms that he will present his thank-offerings to God (v 12). How easy do you find it to praise God in times of persecution or challenge? I wonder if this is one of the psalms Jesus reflected on as he talked and thought about the way he was being pursued by enemies who wanted to kill him. Have you ever had to keep going despite the opposition? How did you handle that?

Such persecution and opposition still happen today. A missionary had been through tough times. In a brutal attack her husband and two sons were killed. Though she pronounced forgiveness to the perpetrators, life was not easy. Haunting memories and questions kept coming back to her. When her faith was tossed like a roller coaster, she would always return to the promise in Psalm 56:11 – 'in God I trust and am not afraid'. She drew strength from knowing that God does not overlook our misery and he keeps count of our tears (v 8).

When I am afraid, I put my trust in you. In God, whose word I praise – in God I trust and am not afraid. What can mere mortals do to me?

Psalm 56:3,4

RESPOND

Pray: 'Help me, Lord, to be aware that when I shed tears you are there by my side and I can trust in you.'

Bible in a year: Isaiah 41,42; Hebrews 5

2 Samuel 8–20

Life-changing true stories

Storytelling: what a gift, for those who skilfully tell stories and for those of us who excitedly hear them! Just now, I'm reading Dickens' *Great Expectations*, and I'm absolutely loving being immersed in the first half of the nineteenth century. Some personalities and motivations don't change!

About the writer
Terry Clutterham

Having been on the staff of SU England and Wales for nearly 30 years, Terry now lives with his wife Sue in Norfolk. They both help train children's leaders in their local church, but at other times Terry enjoys reading, writing, visiting historical sites and entertaining their young grandsons, and has recently got back to playing the recorder for the first time in 35 years – Terry and Sue are currently on pretty good terms with their neighbours!

The book of 2 Samuel may have been compiled during the exile of God's people but written earlier, as the events unfolded. It tells the true story of the nation of Israel around 1,000 BC and especially, in this series of readings, of the life events and person of King David.

Try reading or listening to chapters 8 to 20 in one sitting. We may not enjoy all we hear, but it will give us a much better grasp of all that's going on.

The exquisite storytelling draws us deeply in to thinking about some of the big themes that are as relevant to our own lives as they were to David's. Through our readings, we'll reflect on God's story (What is he planning? What has he promised? What is he doing? What does he want?) and David's story. (To what extent does his life reflect God's nature?) We'll also have a go at telling our own story (What is God doing with us now? Where might he want to take us next?), bringing it to the Lord in prayer.

Ready for some life-changing true story-hearing and -telling?

Monday 22 September

2 Samuel 8:1–18

Devoted

PREPARE

Reflect: 'You are not your own; you were bought at a price' (1 Corinthians 6:19,20). The price was Jesus' blood. Thank him who gave everything for you.

READ

2 Samuel 8:1–18

EXPLORE

Maybe we'll struggle with this part of David's story. We want to love and applaud him, because we know he's a 'good guy', 'a man after my own heart', says God (Acts 13:22), but here we find him slaughtering tens of thousands of soldiers (including some through what seems like a cruel kind of Russian roulette, v 2), crippling horses (v 4) and carrying off tons of his enemies' gold, silver and bronze (vs 7–10). To us, these actions seem abhorrent.

However, if we look more closely, we see that somehow God is right at the heart of everything. God's story is that he wants security for his people (2 Samuel 7:10,11), and David ensures this happens. The Lord is behind his success (vs 6,14), and David dedicates his spoils of war to the Lord (vs 7,11,12). Externally securing Israel's borders, he's God's man for the job (v 14); internally he further strengthens the nation with good, structured government (vs 16–18). However it looks, David is 'doing what was just and right for all his people' (v 15).

However tough and messy the events, challenges and relationships of our daily lives, Jesus' devotion to us inspires us to stay devoted to finding the 'just and right', Jesus-glorifying way through it all.

> The LORD gave David victory wherever he went.
>
> **2 Samuel 8:6b**

RESPOND

Try telling God your own story now, letting him know just how much you love him and reflecting on your attempt to live with him right at the heart of everything. What might he be saying to you in response?

Bible in a year: Isaiah 43,44; Hebrews 6

Tuesday 23 September

2 Samuel 11:1–27

Distracted

PREPARE

'I will listen to what God the LORD says; he promises peace to his people, his faithful servants – but let them not turn to folly' (Psalm 85:8). Relax, knowing that you're at peace with the Lord as you come to listen to his Word.

READ

2 Samuel 11:1–27

EXPLORE

With peace and success can come complacency, a belief in our own invincibility. In this moment of David's story he wants what he wants, and why not? Doesn't he deserve it? It all starts with a distracted glance from the palace roof (v 2), but it leads to David forgetting other people, God and the holiness in his people that the Lord desires (v 27).

A constant theme in God's true story has been that his people should reflect who he is to those around them who don't know him. God identifies so fully with his people that their reputation becomes his. (He still does this with the church today.) I wonder how safe God's reputation is with *us*. God even gave special instructions that the king shouldn't 'turn from the law to the right or to the left' (Deuteronomy 17:20). No wonder David wants to keep his sin quiet!

Most of us keep quiet about *our* sins too. Generally we don't post, stream or chat about them. But of course 'Nothing in all creation is hidden from God's sight' (Hebrews 4:13). So this frees us up amazingly to tell him all about them.

But the thing David had done displeased the LORD.

2 Samuel 11:27b

RESPOND

'Be holy because I, the LORD your God, am holy' (Leviticus 19:2). Hear God say these words to you and examine your life story before him. Thank him that 'we have been made holy through the sacrifice of the body of Jesus Christ once for all' (Hebrews 10:10).

Bible in a year: Isaiah 45,46; Psalm 107

Wednesday 24 September

2 Samuel 12:1–25

Devastated

PREPARE

Thank God for all the great people, things and experiences he has given you, and especially for forgiveness and new life in Jesus.

READ

2 Samuel 12:1–25

EXPLORE

Story is powerful! Nathan's story from God hits home with David. Can you remember a time when words from God stopped you in your tracks?

Initially outraged at the horrific injustice the rich man perpetrates (vs 5,6), David is devastated, then contrite, when God points out that the real guilty party is David himself (v 7). His acts of adultery, murder and therefore unbelievable meanness, in spite of God's overwhelming generosity (v 8), are abhorrent to God. From here on, David's story will be one of strife and heartache (v 11). An epidemic of sinfulness will spread through David's family and nation, the consequence of his abuse of power and string of poor choices.

In God's story sin is always taken very seriously. Here God calls what David does 'despising' him and his word (vs 9,10). So, it's not just a casual slip-up then! Of the 'six things the LORD hates, seven that are detestable to him' (Proverbs 6:16–19), it seems to me that David commits them all! So how amazing it is that through Nathan God still tells him, 'The LORD has taken away your sin' (v 13), and even more so, that Jesus 'takes away the sin of the world' (John 1:29).

Nathan replied, 'The LORD has taken away your sin. You are not going to die.'

2 Samuel 12:13b

RESPOND

Tell God your own story of struggle with sin. Confess and hear him say he forgives you.

Bible in a year: Isaiah 47,48; Hebrews 7

Thursday 25 September
2 Samuel 15:1–12

Diminished

PREPARE

'The Sovereign Lord has opened my ears; I have not been rebellious, I have not turned away' (Isaiah 50:5). Pray for attentiveness to what he has to say to you today.

READ

2 Samuel 15:1–12

EXPLORE

Handsome Absalom, David's third son, aims for popularity with the ordinary people. One day, he hopes, he'll lead them in an uprising against his father and grab the crown for himself. For now, he's letting everyone know he's 'royal' (vs 1,6) and builds his reputation by getting down to the people's level (v 2), by applauding their claims to justice (v 3) and by massaging their egos (v 5). Absalom being a very slick operator, the people simply fall in line behind him (v 6). Gradually, subtly and for a very long time (v 7), Absalom diminishes David's role and credibility in his people's eyes.

In God's story, he has chosen David as king: 'I have chosen David to rule my people Israel' (1 Kings 8:16). David is God's man. By undermining his role, Absalom is working against God's plans. While the words of Psalm 2:1–3 ring true for the surrounding nations bent on doing Israel harm, Absalom is also playing his part in plotting from within 'against the Lord and against his anointed' (Psalm 2:2).

Whoever walks in integrity walks securely.

Proverbs 10:9a

RESPOND

As part of your own story, share with God how your heart aches when you see his glory on the earth diminished by people's selfish ambition. What are you thinking of in particular? And what from scripture does God want to say to you in response?

Bible in a year: Isaiah 49,50; Hebrews 8

Friday 26 September

2 Samuel 15:13–29

Determined

PREPARE

'Take my moments and my days; let them flow in endless praise.'* Will you praise endlessly? Do at least a bit of it now!

READ

2 Samuel 15:13–29

EXPLORE

After resting on his laurels and inadvertently letting Absalom make a bid for the crown, David wakes up to what's actually happening (v 13). Suddenly he's on the case again with his role and with God. David's story isn't over yet, although the country folk watching him think it may be (v 23). No, David emerges with fresh determination. Wise call follows wise call. Did you spot them in today's verses? If not, take another look.

David recognises and acts on the Lord's sovereignty, knowing he's at work. This is primarily God's story. First, with his loyal supporters and soldiers, he strategically and compassionately leaves Jerusalem, so the city isn't trashed and the people slaughtered (though, horribly, the ten concubines are left to their fate, v 16). Next, he generously gives permission for the Gittites to leave (though they don't) – it's not their battle, after all (vs 19–22). And David refuses to use the Ark as a kind of personal protection device (v 25) because he knows God is with him everywhere he goes – it's all in the Lord's hands (v 26).

When it looks as if *he's* finished too, Jesus makes right call after right call… all the way to the cross. Knowledge of God's sovereignty makes the hardest path possible. It's when Jesus knows it's time for him to 'leave this world and go to the Father' (John 13:1) that he picks up a towel and washes feet.

'Let him do to me whatever seems good to him.'

2 Samuel 15:26b

RESPOND

Reflect on Psalm 71:5. Tell the Lord your own story of times when you did all you could but in the end just had to rely on his knowing best. How did things turn out?

*'Take My Life and Let It Be', Frances Ridley Havergal, 1836–79

Bible in a year: Isaiah 51,52; Hebrews 9

Saturday 27 September
2 Samuel 18:1–18

Disobeyed

PREPARE

Read Psalm 131:1, and come to your Bible time today in humility, waiting on the Lord.

READ

2 Samuel 18:1–18

EXPLORE

Some Bible passages leave us with more questions than answers. For me, this is one of them. I understand all the words and can follow the storyline, but it's with the motivations of people that I struggle, and with trying to see God's story in it all. How was the reading for you?

The first five verses are fine – Absalom is trying to kill David, so his troops advise the king to stay in the city (v 3). Complete sense. And David, being a loving father in spite of his son's desire to murder him, wants his army commanders to treat Absalom gently – that is, not kill him (v 5). But they disobey and do kill Absalom, and that's where my questions begin.

If Joab is so loyal to David, why doesn't he do as the king asks and treat Absalom gently (v 14)? Since David's order is made very publicly (v 5), why does Joab risk his position and possibly his life by disobeying it? Does he think that he knows better than the king, that killing Absalom is the only sure way of making sure he doesn't cause more trouble? And what sort of commander would drop one of his troops right in it (v 13)? And why treat the king's son's body so disrespectfully (v 17)?

However much *isn't* clear, what *is* clear is that, with Absalom gone, David now has no obvious heir. So has God's plan for the house of David fallen in a heap? And not just the plan for the next king in line, but what about God's promise to 'establish the throne of his kingdom for ever' (2 Samuel 7:13)? Well, come on – what do *you* think?

> Israel, put your hope in the LORD both now and for evermore.
>
> **Psalm 131:3**

RESPOND

Pray: 'Lord, today I'm puzzled, but thank you for your Word.'

Bible in a year: Isaiah 53,54; Psalms 108,109

Sunday 28 September

Psalm 57

Delivered

PREPARE

If you plotted your life of faith on a graph, would you say you're living at a high point (joyful and praising) or a low point (sorrowful and crying out for help)? Tell the Lord why.

READ

Psalm 57

EXPLORE

The title of the psalm tells us David, in an earlier period of his life, is hiding from Saul 'in a cave'. However, if we glance through the verses again, we'll see just how appropriate they sound for David's later situation with Absalom.

Psalms being songs, this one seems to start softly but with dark undertones, growing louder and more confident. It suddenly dips again at verse 4, before the crescendo of praise in verse 5. The cycle restarts, first low and mysterious (v 6), then rising to the final crashing climax in verse 11. The Lord will deliver him. When David remembers all the Lord is and all he does, gradually he raises his voice and we can imagine him lifting his head: O God, all glory to you, everywhere!

The Lord draws me out of myself too so that I realise it's all about him – he has 'mercy' (v 1), is my 'refuge' (v 1), is the 'Most High' (v 2), 'saves me' (v 3) and showers me with 'his love and his faithfulness' (v 3). I've started here to list the good news about the Lord in this psalm, but can you go from verse 4 and draw out the rest?

And suppose 'those who hotly pursue me', the 'lions', 'ravenous beasts' and horrendous, spear-toothed 'men' (vs 3,4) could represent all 'the devil's schemes' to defeat Christians (Ephesians 6:11,12)? Enjoy reading the psalm again in the light of the extraordinary rescue Jesus brought us by his death.

Be exalted, O God, above the heavens; let your glory be over all the earth.

Psalm 57:5

RESPOND

Now turn your discoveries into a time of praise to the Lord.

Bible in a year: Isaiah 55,56; Hebrews 10

Monday 29 September

2 Samuel 18:19–21,31–33; 19:1–8

Distraught

PREPARE

Lay before the Lord anything in your or your family's life that is preoccupying you and perhaps weighing heavily. Remember, 'my help comes from the LORD, the Maker of heaven and earth' (Psalm 121:2).

READ

2 Samuel 18:19–21,31–33; 19:1–8

EXPLORE

Cushite messenger: 'You're free of threat!' David: 'But what about Absalom?' Messenger: 'Erm...' Result? Even though Absalom has been trying to kill him (17:12), David is naturally distraught at the loss of his son (18:33). Another bitter moment in David's story. In fact he gets so caught up in his own grief that he neglects his royal, God-given duties... That is, until, shrewdly, Joab jolts him out of it (19:5–7). Then suddenly he's back being the king God anointed him to be (19:8). We can't just abandon who God has made us and what he has given us to do.

In God's story, there's no 'slumber nor sleep' for him (Psalm 121:4), nor the relinquishing of his responsibilities as the 'LORD your God' (2 Samuel 18:28). 'If we are faithless, he remains faithful, for he cannot disown himself' (2 Timothy 2:13) – he is our good and faithful God, always.

As we discover in Psalm 89:3,4, there's a lot of 'forever-ness', including around King David, that God has to work on!

'The LORD has vindicated you today by delivering you from the hand of all who rose up against you.'

2 Samuel 18:31b

RESPOND

Tell God your own story of times when you were so in need yourself that you almost felt like giving up on faith. Be thankful that he never fails or forgets – he 'will watch over your coming and going both now and for evermore' (Psalm 121:8).

Bible in a year: Isaiah 57,58; Hebrews 11

Tuesday 30 September

2 Samuel 19:9–18,39–43; 20:1,2

Decisive

PREPARE

Enjoy quiet, if you can. In God's story you and the Lord are at peace, together for ever. What do you want to say to him before setting off with today's reading?

READ

2 Samuel 19:9–18,39–43; 20:1,2

EXPLORE

This part of David's story sees him attempting to regain people's support after their loyalty transferred to Absalom. David must return to Jerusalem now, the people demand, and take control of things again. But with all David has been through, notice his extraordinary generosity of spirit. Rather than punishing Amasa, Absalom's general, he makes him commander of his own army (19:13). Shimei seeks forgiveness for pelting David and his officials with rocks when they were escaping from Jerusalem earlier (16:6–8; 19:19,20). David responds to Shimei's plea – 'May the king put it out of his mind' (19:19). There's no recrimination of any sort by the king (19:23), and of Joab and his murder of the king's son there's not a word. Despite Israel's and Judah's bickering about which of them has the strongest case for the privilege of bringing David back (19:40–43), there's no response recorded from David.

The decisive, peaceful way in which David deals with Absalom's rebellion and its consequences is remarkable. Even if it's tactical, to reintroduce peace and calm to troubled times, the powerful king could have chosen another way.

And what peace another King so generously and decisively brought into our lives: '... since we have been justified through faith, we have peace with God through our Lord Jesus Christ ...' (Romans 5:1).

Forgive as the Lord forgave you.

Colossians 3:13b

RESPOND

Thank God that, in your own story and through Jesus, you have known his forgiveness for far more than you have ever forgiven other people.

Bible in a year: Isaiah 59,60; Psalms 110,111